Kathleen Harvey Harshberger

Praise for *Etiquette Still Matters*

"Kathleen Harshberger presents the often thorny rules of etiquette and protocol with skill and humor. Make no mistake though: she knows all the rules, and she takes the guesswork out of the process. I highly recommend this book!"

Dr. Raymond Smoot
Chairman, Union Bankshares Corporation
CEO Emeritus, Virginia Tech Foundation

"Ever confident and graceful in her seminars in Istanbul or Los Angeles, Ms. Kathleen Harshberger never fails to bring her special touch and charm to the field of etiquette and protocol."

Prof. Dr. Murat Ferman
President, Beykent University, Istanbul, Turkey

"For over 15 years, Kathleen Harshberger has had a profound effect on our dining program at Radford University. From her impactful training sessions for our catering staff to the partnering and creating of our etiquette program we offer to graduating seniors each year, she has continued to have a positive influence on our students and staff. She has reached thousands of students with her insightful, humorous, and educational approach to help them get ready for the "what next' moments after earning their degrees. She has been a tremendous asset, friend and leader for our dining experiences. Putting it all on paper to share in this book is exactly what you would expect from Kathleen!"

Michael Lannon
VP of Operations, Chartwells

"No dry collection of directives, these! Instead, Ms. Harshberger offers vibrant pointers in her efforts to rescue us from committing a variety of social misdemeanors . . . and some felonies! To this task she brings sense and sensitivity, élan and humor.

Dr. Giovanni Chimienti
San Diego, California
Author: Italia! A half-century of travels in Italy

"When I met Kathleen Harshberger ten years ago, I would have said that etiquette was simply knowing appropriate table manners. But I have learned from her that etiquette, of course, is broader than that. Etiquette, or protocol, is the skill that allows us to be confident and at ease in any social or professional setting. Kathleen imparts that skill in her book, and you will find it to be an invaluable resource in being prepared for the social and professional circumstances that might otherwise confound you. You will find Kathleen's ability to personalize the real-life situations she has encountered and observed make her recommendations and suggestions easy to apply."

Ed Lawhorn
Former New River Valley Market Executive
Atlantic Union Bank, Christiansburg

"Fantastic! Kathleen Harshberger has written a book that coaches us on the do's and don't of proper business etiquette. We all want to do the right things to be successful — now we know what those things are!"

Joe W. Meredith, Ph.D.
President, Virginia Tech Corporate Research Center, Inc.

"For years, Kathleen Harvey Harshberger's articles in Valley Business FRONT answered all of our questions (including those questions we did not realize we had) regarding etiquette and protocol in politics and incivility, diplomacy, hosting guests and being the guest — and my favorite — Phubbing. How wonderful that all of the articles are contained in one book — informative and delightful — a treasure that will be referenced and enjoyed for years to come."

Sandra C. Davis
Owner, BCR Real Estate and Property Management

"WOW! Here's a new book covering everything anyone needs to know about business etiquette and protocol. Leave it up to an expert in this area, Kathleen Harshberger, to put it all together for us. This is something that is needed in our current business world. Kathleen has been teaching and writing about this subject for a pretty long time. She knows this stuff. It is really time for all of us to take a look at how we mix with people, not only in business, but in our daily lives. This new book is put together in such a manner that it provides easy reading and understanding. It is a collection of a variety of articles written by Kathleen over the years, and it is all very current. It should be required reading in all colleges and schools."

Howard Feiertag
Virginia Tech Pamplin College of Business
Department of Hospitality and Tourism Management

ETIQUETTE

Still

MATTERS

Dedication

To my husband, Dr. Richard F. Harshberger
"the wind beneath my wings"
and to the memory of our dearly loved daughter, Katy

Foreword

To open this delightful book is like being a guest in the author's home. The experience is guaranteed to be welcoming and warm, and proper, but by no means fussy. These same words typify Kathleen Harshberger's approach to hosting, and more to the point in the instance of this book, her approach to teaching etiquette and protocol.

Furthermore, the title "Etiquette Still Matters" could not be more apt, as in these pages Kathleen presents a breezy and accessible guide to how aspects of social and professional interaction still profoundly affect us all on a daily and very personal basis.

While acknowledging the modes of generations past, Kathleen not only capitalizes on her excellent training in this subject matter, but also brings a wealth of experience accrued through teaching and international travel. This goes a long way toward the principal appeal of this book—it is intensely practical, it is very contemporary, it is for now.

Kathleen's approach upholds a standard and at the same time illustrates that rules for social behavior need to be flexible. In summary, it is a marvelous mixture of common sense and situation, of tradition and anecdote that, far from being a dry seminar, is like a festive evening at the Harshberger home. It is refreshing, enlightening, and enjoyable. And might I add, in a world far too often given to incivility and vulgarity, this valuable volume reminds us why etiquette matters still matter.

Wesley A. Young, MFA
Professor of Theatre, Radford University

Contents

A Note about the arrangement and formatting: This book includes a compilation of business journal columns published between 2011 and 2018. They are not presented here in chronological order of publication; but rather assembled together under similar classifications. Original entries are published by Valley Business FRONT and available for review in the archives at www.vbFRONT.com.

Introduction

What a great idea.

That was the first reaction that popped in my head when the notion of this book arose. Let's compile the etiquette columns Kathleen Harvey Harshberger has been providing my business journal for these past eight years. After all, her column is one of the most popular components of our ongoing lineup; and we get more input on these "matters of etiquette" than any other regular feature. I've received letters about her column. I've had readers run up to me and suggest topics for her to address. And I've had numerous patrons tell me they use her material in their own professions—either to adjust their own behaviors or to share best practices with fellow associates or staff. Apparently, it's cool to be civil.

The second reaction that popped in my head?

What an honor.

I remember my first phone call to Kathleen. Never have I felt more reassured by an introduction than I did after hanging up the telephone that afternoon. Little did I know, Kathleen was practicing etiquette at the highest level of perfection from my very first conversation! All I knew was that I had "discovered" exactly the right columnist for our business journal in this regard.

Kathleen has the touch of elegance and grace without the stuffiness or pretentiousness. Our readers are going to benefit greatly from this, I thought. And indeed, we all have.

One aspect about this book you will find intriguing: There are topics that are certainly relevant to the day they were submitted. There are also nuances mentioned and specific references that apply to the moment they were submitted. Won't that affect the timeliness? we might inquire. Won't that be irrelevant for today's reader? Not at all. In fact, Kathleen even reverses that concern herself by presenting etiquette "rules" from the 13th Century!

Etiquette, civility, well-mannered behavior endures. Or at least it should.

Which brings us to the purpose of this book. I believe we need to put into practice *more* etiquette. In today's workplace. And in our society at large. This book helps that effort.

Imagine your day tomorrow if you and everyone you engaged improved our attitudes, our behaviors, and yes, our very mannerisms—just a smidge. Would it make a difference?

It's worth a try.

Tom Field, Publisher / Editor
Valley Business FRONT

PLEASURE TO MEET YOU

Effective handshaking >

The venerable handshake is not only acceptable at a time when most touching isn't, but it is preferred.

Handshaking, which is the accepted standard for initial greeting in business around the world, goes back to ancient times. One theory says that extending a weaponless right hand indicated goodwill and peaceful intentions. A ninth century B.C. bas-relief shows the Assyrian king, Shalmaneser, shaking hands with a Babylonian leader, possibly to seal an alliance. Homer, the epic poet, in his "Iliad" and "Odyssey" described handshakes as signs of trust, and symbols of clasped hands are even found on Roman coins.

A woman did not shake hands until around the Edwardian era, and even then she remained seated. Gender issues do not apply in contemporary business. Today's professional woman stands and shakes hands just like her male counterpart – a huge departure from the old etiquette when women remained seated and offered their hand first.

What is an effective handshake in the 21st century? Here are some tips to remember in both your business and social worlds.

- Be ready to shake hands.
- It is considered rude and disrespectful to refuse to shake another's hand.
- Unless you have a medical reason not to, always use your right hand.
- Hold your glass in your left hand to avoid offering an icy hand.
- Smile, make eye contact, and offer a firm hand shake.
- Be aware of when to let go – a handshake that lingers can be taken as anxious, or even creepy

Like body language, our handshake offers clues about how we feel about ourselves and about others. Take note the next time you shake hands:

- Dead Fish: possibly the most unpleasant; this is usually the sign of a lack of energy and low self-esteem.
- Brush off: A quick grip and rapid release; if you feel you are being marginalized by this handshake, you would be right!
- Two handed handshake: Used by politicians to try to convey friendliness and honesty. Be careful though, if the hand wanders up your arm, he or she is looking for something from you! This handshake is also used by ministers when consoling a bereaved person. No matter the situation, this handshake is not appropriate in the business world.
- Finger holder: a sign of insecurity, saying "keep your distance."
- Bone Crusher: this is designed to intimidate you.
- Perspiring palms: a sign of a nervous person – try to be kind!

Some people have a phobia about shaking hands and are afraid of catching germs from others. If you have that concern, try to remember that almost everything you touch has been touched before by someone else – plates, glasses, cups, door handles – the list is endless. And think of all the hands that politicians shake. What's their secret? In this modern day, it is anti-bacterial hand cleaner!

Windows to the soul >

Proper eye contact varies widely,
depending on the culture. Be sure you
get it right. You could inadvertently
offend.

When Elizabeth Taylor died, much was written about her beautiful violet eyes and how they captivated those with whom she spoke. While I was a student at Radford University, Ms. Taylor visited the campus to campaign for her husband, Senator John Warner. When I looked into those violet eyes, I realized it was more than the color of her eyes that captivated; rather it was how she used those eyes. When she talked to me, she held my eyes completely, and didn't look around to see who else was watching or listening. Flattering and captivating. You bet. I never forgot it.

In our culture, we typically make direct eye contact around 50 percent of the time. If we don't make proper eye contact, we could be considered sneaky, untrustworthy or even lying. On the other hand, if we hold a gaze too long, we can intimidate and be considered overconfident, rude, aggressive, or even creepy!

Although proper eye contact is necessary for social and business communications, some of us have a hard time doing this. I tell my clients if they are shy, to look at the spot between the eyebrows and it will appear they are making eye contact.

The 50 percent standard doesn't necessarily hold true in other cultures. In some Middle Eastern traditions eye contact is very long, lingering, and intense. This can intimidate Westerners, so if you are doing business in those cultures be aware, and resist the urge to break eye contact. We share a language with the English, but some of our habits are quite different. While we make direct eye contact when speaking, our British colleague will often look away while speaking, and then look at you directly to indicate that it is your turn to talk.

In Japan, direct eye contact could be a sign of disrespect. Children are taught to lower their eyes when speaking to a superior or an older person. Although experienced Japanese professionals have studied Western business and cultural practices, and made direct eye contact effortlessly. We could take a lesson here, and study all cultures if we wish to excel in the global marketplace.

Our eyes reveal a great deal about ourselves and others. Eyes reveal love, happiness, sadness, bitterness, hatred, amusement, sincerity, trust, distrust; in fact the whole range of human emotions. So let's be aware of what our eyes are telling others. We might be sending a very different message from what our words are saying.

Business cards:
A perspective >

A lesson from the Japanese gives
this humble business accoutrement a
little status and style.

Our modern day business cards are the legacy of two types of cards that were prevalent in the 17th, 18th and 19th Centuries. By 17th Century England, the use of trade cards was widespread.

Merchants put advertising and maps on their cards—early marketing. During the 18th and 19th Centuries, calling cards were the norm. "Calling" was another word for visiting, and presenting these cards became a ritualized, complicated social obligation.

Until a decade or so ago, we didn't think much about our business cards. We handed them out willy-nilly, with no thought to form and style. It took the Japanese businessman to demonstrate to us the importance of properly presenting and receiving the business card. Today, let's examine what business cards are really all about, and what they say about us and the business we represent.

Our business cards say who we are and they represent our business or profession. We want to present ourselves with confidence and authority in all aspects of our professional life, from the way we dress to the way we conduct ourselves in a dining situation. Our business card is just one more way in which we show we know what we are doing professionally.

A good business card is one that clearly states your business and your contact information. Some professions, such as the legal profession, will have a more conservative card, perhaps white with black printing. Other professions, such as the graphic arts, can get away with a more arresting visual impact. Others might have a logo on their card to aid in branding. The important thing to remember, though, is that the printing be easily readable, and the card not too fussy.

- Never present a card that is wrinkled, stained or torn; that's not nice.
- Carry your cards in a good quality leather card case; never plastic.
- Keep a supply of your cards handy at all times—you look foolish
  when you can't produce one.
- Don't hand out cards indiscriminately at private social events. It's tacky.
- Don't distribute cards like you're dealing from a deck!
  Makes one look brash and shallow.
- Give your card to the receptionist each time you visit—pays dividends.
- Junior executives should not press their card on senior executive—wait until asked.
- Present your card with the print facing the recipient—you've already read it.
- When receiving a card, take time to read it—give value to the giver.
- Don't write notes on the card in the presence of the giver—very unprofessional.

Business cards are one of your smallest business expenses, but they can have a significant impact on your bottom line.

Networking and charisma >

Arming yourself against anxiety can
help you in those social situations.

Everyone has a favorite resolution at the new year: exercise, healthy eating, learning a new skill. The list is endless. In the professional world, at this time, we often vow to make more contacts and do more networking. So let's talk about networking and how charisma plays a part in the process.

Many professionals dread networking and, if you are one of those, it might help to remember that: 40 percent of all adults live with social anxiety, and 75 percent of adults experience anxiety at the very thought of entering a gathering that is full of strangers. It does not matter if the occasion is a social or business. So if you feel nervous when walking into a networking situation, remember you are not alone. Most people there are just as anxious as you.

To arm ourselves for these situations, developing a little charisma will help. Have you ever noticed that some people seem to command attention simply by walking into a room? What's their secret? Are they born with that certain something that draws people to them? That something is often called charisma, a magnetic appeal. The word is rooted in Latin and Greek (aren't they all?) and refers to a grace or favor, which was considered a divine gift from God. Remember, rulers throughout history have maintained absolute power by asserting their "divine" rights.

No doubt about it, those with a high level of charisma will be listened to and respected as leaders. Who are these people who have that certain indefinable something? We often see it in actors, sports heroes, models, business leaders, and politicians. In my Business Etiquette seminars, I often ask the question, "Are these people born with that magnetism or do they learn it?" The truth is that very few of us are born with charisma. Fortunately, the gift of drawing people to you is a quality that can be developed, and if you want to succeed in the professional world, you have good reasons to do just that. Consider what it is and what it is not:

- Charisma is not showing off.

- Charisma is not just reserved for the famous and celebrated.

- Charisma is a quality that can be developed.

- Charisma helps in any situation where you need or want to influence other people.

- Charisma is a tool that can help us in leading a team involved in
  project management, problem solving, innovation and pioneering.

Later, we're going to talk about projecting confidence and authority—and charisma—as you make an entrance and work the room.

Making an entrance and making it count >

If showing up is such a big part
of success, you'll want to make sure
you show up right.

Have you ever noticed that some people command attention simply by walking into a room? They make an entrance and they make it count. Let's look at some strategies that can help you do the very same thing.

Be prepared! No matter the event, know your reason for attending. In other words, know your objective, and prepare accordingly.

To make an effective entrance: maintain good posture; do not rush; walk slowly and purposefully past the door, and move a step or two to the side so as not to block it; pause for a moment before continuing into the room. This allows you to scan your surroundings and see to whom you want to talk and, more importantly – because most people watch the entrance – it allows others to see you. This is when you make your first impression.

Be aware of your facial expression. Enter smiling, or if you can't manage that, with a pleasant look on your face. This lets others know that you are friendly and approachable.

You already know that good eye contact, a firm handshake, a smile, and being able to introduce yourself and others easily are tools that can take you far. Now it's time to use them as you mingle and "work the room."

Keep your glass in your left hand, so that your right hand is free for handshakes. While you certainly want to enjoy the event, your purpose is not just to have fun; it is to further your career objectives. Enjoy a libation and a nibble or two, but remember your purpose; it shouldn't be only about eating and drinking!

Prepare a few topics to chat about, because small talk breaks the ice. Now there's nothing "small" about small talk, and all good conversationalists know this. It's the tool they use to assess whether or not they want to move on to the next level of a relationship, albeit business or social.

Focus on the other person, and listen. Listening intently to another is a compliment. Avoid interrupting two people engaged in deep conversation. Their body language should clue you in to that, and interrupting them would be rude.

Be strategic when offering your business card. Your cards represent you and your business, so best not to fling them around indiscriminately.

This is not the time to participate in controversial issues. Tread lightly here before jumping into any conversation that includes opinions that may offend. And we all know what I mean!

On leaving: it's just plain tacky to steal away and, make no mistake here, it will be noticed. So leave gracefully after thanking your hosts for a lovely time. Afterwards, follow up with your contacts, and send a nice "thank you" note to your hosts.

You're in My Space! >

Sometimes two IS a crowd,
if you're standing too close.

Have you ever felt uncomfortable because a person is standing too close to you? Or have you been frustrated because you don't seem to be able to "connect" with someone during a conversation because they are standing too far from you? This usually happens with international colleagues, and understanding what you are experiencing may be fundamental to closing a business deal.

The term "proxemics" was originated by the famous anthropologist Edward T. Hall in his seminal book *The Hidden Dimension*, published in 1966. This book studies how space affects humans, and how the space between people can make one feel quite comfortable or quite anxious. There are more than twenty elements of proxemics, but for our purposes we will address the nuances of just personal territory or, if you prefer, "personal space."

Personal territory can be defined as that invisible bubble of space we carry around us that we erect between ourselves and another person. In the United States, as in other cultures, we probably automatically assimilate that knowledge from birth – observing parents, and others. But when we venture abroad, especially in the business arena, we would serve ourselves well to have at least a broad understanding of what is happening in the space between two people.

Let's look at just a few cultures where the proxemics of personal space plays an important role in negotiation:

- Middle Eastern people stand very, very close, often nose to nose! You should resist the urge to step back, as it can be considered insulting to back away from a conversation. Personal Space: Conversation Distances: 8–12 inches

- Americans are conscious of their space, and experience difficulty when standing very close to those of certain cultures. That's when rehearsal before an important meeting comes into play. Personal Space: Conversation Distances: 18–20 inches – think of it as a handshake away.

- The British stand even further away than their American counterparts. Personal Space: Conversation Distances: 24 inches – further than Americans can usually tolerate, unless they understand a little of proxemics.

- Northern Europeans, especially the British, protect the space around them, and touching or moving in too close is an invasion of privacy

Remember, this is only one aspect of proxemics, and I've barely covered it properly here. There is also eye contact, facial expression, nonverbal communication, gender, number of people involved, subject matter and goals of the meeting. So when you venture into the international business arena, remember a working knowledge of proxemics will make you a smart, internationally aware business person.

All about the pause >

Here's a practical technique often overlooked in our effort to perform, produce, and get things completed.

A friend, who knows I conduct etiquette seminars for professionals, asked me for advice on public speaking. I said, "It's all about the pause." Let's talk about the power of a pause in our professional lives, whether speaking in public, making a presentation, or engaging others in a social setting.

Successful people always project the appearance of confidence and authority. I advise my business protocol students to pause briefly in the doorway before entering a meeting or a social gathering. This is a deliberate, purposeful action to make one's presence known. Actors do it, models do it, singers do it, sports figures do it, and so do politicians. As a professional person, so should you.

Some of you are thinking, "I don't want to be noticed!" Think of this, then, as another tool in your professional toolbox. You want to stand out from your competition, and the pause, along with good eye contact and a good handshake, is an additional way of presenting yourself well.

Let's get back to public speaking. Think of the good speakers you have heard, or heard about. Winston Churchill was a master of the pause, so was Martin Luther King, and certainly Steve Jobs.

The speaker who talks quickly without pausing can irritate an audience, in part because it can't easily assimilate verbal information when it is delivered in haste. Speakers who rush through their message are telegraphing nervousness, making their audience nervous and irritable too. They can be considered losers, not leaders.

Think of the speakers that have bored you. They probably spoke in a monotone, giving every word the same weight. If they pause, they usually pause far too long. We've all been tortured by that kind of speaker.

Three reasons why you should master the pause:

- It gives your audience/coworkers a chance to reflect on your message,
  and gives the message time to imprint.
- It gives you the chance to make your point, and also gauge
  the audience's reaction to what you have said.
- It makes you look like a leader and in control.
  Remember you want your audience to hear, understand, respect
  and remember you and your message.

So don't rush. Slow down, and remember the power of the pause. Your message will be remembered longer, and you will gain credibility. You might even gain the reputation for being an excellent speaker!

"The right word may be effective, but no word was ever as effective as a rightly timed pause." — Mark Twain

Soft skills
in the workplace >

Good etiquette can make the
difference between all employees in
general, and the above average.

I attended a gathering of concerned business leaders anxious to promote a resurgence of downtown business. Several complained that, while some new employees came with excellent educations and great technical skills (often called hard skills), many lacked the softer skills.

In my business etiquette seminars I often say that, in this fiercely competitive business arena, soft skills (in other words, good etiquette) are simply another tool you need. While the softer skills and etiquette alone won't get you anywhere, it will give you an extra edge that will make the difference between you and another person who is just as smart and well educated.

I then add that, according to research conducted by Harvard University, The Carnegie Foundation, and The Stanford Research Institute, technical skill and knowledge account for only 15% of the reason we get a job, keep a job, and advance in a job. In other words, 85% of our job success is connected to our diplomatic skills, our people skills, our softer skills. This usually elicits a groan from those who are in the more technical professions (e.g. engineers, accountants, and IT workers). They usually prefer to get from A to Z in a linear fashion, without "wasting time with the niceties" as one participant told me.

The fact remains, though, that we can be the very best in our field, but it will make little difference if we can't get along with our co-workers, our superiors and our clients.

So what are soft skills?

Unlike hard skills which can be measured, soft skills are not easily quantifiable. Yet we all instinctively recognize the person who demonstrates them. Some say that soft skills cannot be taught, that you either have the ability naturally or you don't. This writer disagrees with that notion. Like any other skill, awareness and practice is key here.

Soft skills, or people skills, are sometimes linked with our EQ, or Emotional Intelligence Quotient. It can include traits such as good manners, good communication skills, effective leadership and the ability to positively manage people. Central to Emotional Intelligence is empathy: the ability to understand and feel what another human being is experiencing. I believe that, if you develop that special skill, it can be invaluable in your professional life.

The late, great Barbara Jordan, American lawyer, educator and politician, said "If you're going to play the game properly, you'd better know every rule." An unwritten rule for professional success is to sharpen and use your people skills.

Mingle with
skill and confidence >

Networking... business professionals
are constantly told to do it; but many
still fear or are intimidated by the
very idea.

Many professionals approach the idea of networking with trepidation, even though they know that one- to-one encounters are still considered one of the best ways to generate new business opportunities. Consider the following ways to enjoy your next networking event and negotiate it with skill and confidence.

Prepare for the event. When Benjamin Franklin wrote "By failing to prepare, you are preparing to fail," he probably wasn't thinking about networking, but nevertheless, his observation serves our purpose. Without a plan, all we will probably do is schmooze with colleagues, hang out at the bar, and eat the hors d'oeuvres.

Have your plan in place to promote yourself and your company. How will you describe who you are, and what you do in a quick, interesting way? Practice speaking with confidence, so that you don't stumble your way along.

Expect to have fun and enjoy the event – that way you probably will. While it is in our best interests to behave professionally, it's fine to lighten up and build a connection. It could be by finding a common interest outside of work - sports, theatre, or pets. Note I said "common interest" here. Don't make it all about you.

Try to have positive, meaningful, interactions with potential clients. Don't whisk around the room collecting a pocketful of business cards from people you probably won't follow up with anyway. A business card is an extension of the giver and who he or she is, so treat the card with respect. Look at it and read it before pocketing it.

Listen, listen, and listen. Yes, I know I've written about that before, but it bears repeating. Remember the saying, "When you are interested, you become more interesting?" It's true. So ask sincere questions of people, then stop, and allow them time to speak. I believe this one practice is a very powerful way to engage and interest those with whom you want to connect.

Think about how you can help others. Connect other people in the room to each other, especially those who seem a little lost. Don't have a scarcity mentality and hold onto your contacts like a miser. Steven Covey said: "People with a scarcity mentality tend to see everything in terms of win-lose… The more we develop an abundance mentality, the more we are genuinely happy for the successes [and]…achievements…of others…We believe their success adds to, rather than detracts from, our lives."

So, prepare to have a successful networking event. Expect to have fun. Listen and help others. You may be surprised at the unanticipated positive outcomes!

AT THE TABLE

Dining: The basics >

There are times—like when you're interviewing for a job—when knowing proper table manners can mean success or failure.

"The world was my oyster, but I used the wrong fork!"—Oscar Wilde

In an earlier time proper etiquette at the table was usually taught in the home and in school. However, in these hectic days of work, school, after-school activities, and homework, families no longer sit down regularly at the end of the day to dine together. College graduates and young aspiring executives are often intimidated when they are invited for lunch or dinner as part of the interview process. They should be aware ahead of time that it is usually a test to observe their table manners. The reasoning is that, if a person cannot conduct him or herself easily at the table, and demonstrate a rudimentary knowledge of dining skills, what else is lacking in their education?

Radford University is one of a handful of universities in Virginia that offers its students dining skills training, and I conduct an etiquette dinner there a few times a year. Students, dressed in their "Interview" best, enjoy a four course meal, and I answer questions throughout the meal.

There is a teachable moment here. It is a wonderful thing to see how earnest these young people are, as they balance holding a knife and fork properly, with making pleasant conversation, and absorbing the rules of dining etiquette.

Here are some of the questions, along with my answers, that students often asked:

- How do I seat myself?
  You seat yourself from the right side of the chair.
- When do I pick up my napkin?
  Wait for your host to pick up their napkin before you pick up yours.
- What if I don't like the food?
  You're in the grown up world now! Try everything unless you are allergic
  or have dietary restrictions. If you do have allergies or dietary restrictions,
  it is your responsibility to tell your hosts ahead of time.
- How do I eat soup?
  Spoon soup away from you.
- Can I cut all my food at once?
  Cut and eat only one piece of food at a time.
- What if someone talks to me while I'm eating?
  Take small bites to make swallowing easier.
- How do I treat the wait staff?
  Politely and pleasantly – always!
- How do I eat a roll properly?
  Break a small piece, butter it, and eat it.
- How do I excuse myself from the table?
  Say excuse me; leave your napkin on the chair, and leave.
- When is the meal over?
  When your host places the napkin on the table.
- What's the difference between the American and European style of eating?
  Ah, that's for another time!

Business entertaining >

Remember, it's not about the food,
it's about building the relationship.

Business entertaining is a multi-billion dollar business and represents the largest social activity in the world today. Its roots go back to Greek and Roman times when the ties between personal and professional life were intrinsically bound together. This is still true in some cultures, where business is conducted within a small circle of family or close, trusted friends. In the United States we usually separate the two, and some find business entertaining to be nerve-racking. Since a meal in public provides a backdrop for so many business interactions, let's take some of the guesswork out of the process!

Extending an invitation:

- The host decides restaurant, keeping geography in mind.
  Nobody wants to travel across a busy city for lunch.
- Be precise about the time, place, and purpose of the meeting.
- Be precise about where you meet. I remember sitting for a half hour
  inside the restaurant while my guest waited for me in the lobby.
  Bad form on my part!
- Phone your guest the day before to confirm the date and time.
- Don't let your guest worry about what is appropriate to order.
  Say something like, "The filet mignon here is excellent!" and you
  are letting your guest know it is fine to order a similar item.
- No ifs and's or but's here: the host is responsible for paying for the meal.
- Some men have a problem allowing a woman to pay. If I know that,
  I arrive early and ask the restaurant to run my credit card ahead of time.
- Remember this is about getting to know a potential client on a one to one basis,
  and/or reinforcing a relationship with an existing client.

Accepting an invitation:

- Think about the reasons you are invited: to thank you for prior business,
  to seek advice or information, or to talk about future business opportunities.
  Then prepare ahead of time.
- Remember, it is not about the eating, it is about the meeting.
- Avoid difficult to eat foods: lobster, spaghetti – you know what they are!
- Be prepared to make small talk before getting down to business.
- Unless there is a time constraint, don't discuss business too early.
- After the meal, during desert and coffee, is when most business discussions occur.
- It is the responsibility of the host to decide the timing of a business conversation.
  So if your host wants to jump straight into a discussion you, as the savvy
  professional, will be prepared to do so.

Bon Appetit!

The best dinner guest >

How to make it onto the "A List" is easier than you think.

You're an up and coming professional and you've been invited to your boss's home for dinner. Here's your chance to shine, yet many young (and not so young!) people dread that invitation. Most accomplished hosts know that to make a party successful, they will invite at least one tried and true guest who doesn't go expecting to be entertained. They bring their best self and plan to have a good time.

In Victorian and Edwardian days, dinner parties were elaborate affairs. If you saw the film *Titanic*, you might remember Leonardo DeCaprio's character, as he stared in panic at the myriad of glasses and silverware. "Nothing indicates a well-bred man more than a proper mode of eating. A man may pass muster by dressing well, and may sustain himself tolerably in conversation; but if he be not perfectly at ease with a knife and fork, dinner will betray him." *–Hints on Etiquette*, 1836.

Though, to some, these rules seem a bit archaic, most 19th century manners are still the norm today. A person's breeding, then and now, is on display at the dinner table. People still don't like it when you slurp your soup, or spray food when you talk. Assuming you have mastered proper dining etiquette, what are some of the niceties that makes one a popular and sought after guest?

At a dinner party the host has many duties. So has the guest!

- RSVP promptly. Remember RSVP means respond whether or not you are coming.
- Explain dietary restrictions when you RSVP.
  It is rude to announce a seafood allergy as the bisque is being served.
- Never ask, "Who else is coming?"
- Arrive on time—not too late and not too early.
- Bring a hostess gift. Wine is nice but rather boring.
  Why not chocolates, or flowers that are already arranged?
- Never change the place cards on a table! Very bad form.
- Do not criticize anything—the food, the wine, definitely not your host's children!
- Hold up your end of a conversation, but don't dominate it.
- Have a little tool box of conversational topics to pull out when conversation lags.
- Help smooth awkward moments, especially those associated
  with politics or religion.
- Thank the hosts and (this will get you kudos from your boss's wife!),
  send a thank you note.

Master the above, and you will always be on the "A" list of popular and sought after guests.

Afternoon tea >

For business or pleasure,
consider bringing back the
delights of afternoon tea.

"There are few hours in life more agreeable than the hour dedicated to the ceremony known as afternoon tea."—Henry James

There is something irresistible about a tea party! Whether for business or pleasure, drinking tea with colleagues or friends somehow calms us, creating a soothing, civilized atmosphere. True or not, one legend attributes the discovery of tea to the Chinese emperor, Shen Sun. While resting near a wild tea bush, and sipping hot water, leaves from the bush blew into his container. The emperor drank the water, and thus began mankind's fascination with "taking tea."

Let's segue to England. In the 1650's coffee houses were popular, indeed part of the fabric of everyday life. Tea was for medicinal purposes only, and stocked in pharmacies. By the late 1650's, however, tea started to be brought to the coffee houses and the "taking of tea" became the rage.

Tea drinking was also popular in America, but in December, 1773 something happened in Boston, Massachusetts. England had been heavily taxing tea in the colonies, and those taxes infuriated the colonials. Fifty armed men disguised as Indians attacked three tea ships in Boston Harbor. They hurled 342 chests of tea into the water – "the Boston Tea Party." People began to drink coffee because tea became the symbol of English oppression.

Today, afternoon tea meetings can be a valuable tool in business. Breakfast meetings are difficult to attend, and some say uncivilized! Luncheon meetings break up the day, and many prefer to go home to their families rather than take a chunk of their evening for a dinner meeting. Afternoon tea business meetings are inexpensive, have a finite time frame, and the taking of tea adds a certain courtesy to negotiations.

Internationally, in Turkey for instance, tea is the pre-cursor to doing business. In the sophisticated boutiques in Istanbul, in the stalls of the Covered Bazaar, and in high level negotiations, one socializes and drinks tea before business.

The traditional time for afternoon tea is 4 o'clock, although any time between three and five o'clock works well. Typically, there are three separate courses – savories, scones, and sweets. Caution! Unlike its name suggests, high tea is not a fancy tea. It is a simple, hearty, sit-down meal that originated during the industrial revolution of the 19th century. Calling afternoon tea "high tea" is considered very bad form.

Afternoon tea is about socializing and enjoying colleagues and friends. So step away from the hum-drum, and plan afternoon tea for your next business meeting.

"I got nasty habits...I drink tea at three."—Mick Jagger

Great service expectations >

Dining experiences are enhanced when proper tableside service is practiced.

For the past few decades, there has been a great deal of emphasis in the food industry on serving quality foods that are not only delicious, but a delight to the eye. Witness the rise of food networks and the fascination many have with watching cooking shows. Chefs compete with each other under extraordinary time constraints to produce culinary delights with an artistic touch.

Now what about when the meal is handed over to the wait staff? In many restaurants, dining can be spoiled by inexperienced and badly trained servers. As guests in a good restaurant, we should expect that those who wait on us to:

- Remember the three "P"s and be Poised, Polite, Professional.
- Observe the basics of good grooming and personal hygiene.
- Not chew gum – Oh, no!
- Handle tableware and silverware correctly.
- Handle plates by spreading fingers under and placing thumb on the edge.
- Pick up silverware by the handles: never touching a fork by the tines,
  a knife by the blade, or a spoon by the bowl.
- Handle cups (are you ready for this?) by the handles and glasses by the stems.
- Smile and make eye contact.
- Say "Welcome" or "Good evening" — not "Hi, how are ya?"
- Identify the host or hostess.
- Avoid slang and informality, addressing guests as "Sir" or "Ma-am"—
  not "folks" or "guys."
- Serve food with the left hand at the guest's left. (It is rude to serve food
  with your right hand to the guest's left – that's called "backhanding.)
- Serve water, wine and hot beverages with the right hand at the guest's right.
- Serve beverages correctly. There are two schools of thought about
  serving beverages: stationery (leaving glass on the table) or lifting to pour.
  Stationery method is more correct, and needs practice.
- Never reach across the guests to serve anything. This is considered lazy
  service and will land them in the Wait Staff Hall of Shame!
- Realize that "No problem!" is an attitude, not a response to "Thank you!"
- Not ask, "Are you still working on this?" but rather "May I remove your plate?"
- Remove plates, silverware and glasses from the right side of the guest.
- Present the check with a smile.
- Bid us goodbye.

If you are a guest, consider giving feedback – positive or negative – based on the above. Who knows? Maybe your input will improve your service next time!

The timelessness
of table manners >

Dining etiquette hasn't
changed much over the years.

I ran into a book called *Manners and Morals of Victorian America*, compiled by Wayne Erbsen and published in 2009 by Native Ground Books and Music, Ashville, N.C. It is fun to read because some of the advice is hopelessly out-of-date. Not dining etiquette, though! The advice, often written in an amusing style, is just about as current today as when it was written. All of the quotes date between 1881 and 1910.

Sensible Table Manners:
- Do not play with the utensils.
- Do not put your elbows on the table.
- Do not talk loudly or boisterously.
- Be cheerful in conduct and conversation.
- Never, if possible, cough or sneeze at the table.
- Do not bend the head low down over the plate.
  (The food should go to the mouth, not the mouth to the food.)
- Never make a noise while eating.
- Do not open the mouth while chewing, but keep the lips closed.
- Do not talk when the mouth is full.
- Never put fruit or bon-bons in your pocket to carry them from the table.
- It is not necessary to show persons how you masticate your food.
- When you are at the table do not show restlessness by fidgeting in your seat.
- Do not introduce disgusting or unpleasant topics of conversation.

Bad Table Manners:
- Tips chair back.
- Eats with mouth too full.
- Feeds dog at the table.
- Holds his knife improperly.
- Engages in arguments at mealtime.
- Lounges on the table.
- Brings a cross child to the table (well that's gone out the window!)
- Drinks from a saucer and laps the last drop.
- Comes to the table in shirt sleeves, (see etiquette quiz below).
- Picks his teeth with his fingers. The habit which some have of holding
  one hand over the mouth, does not avoid the vulgarity of teeth picking at the table
- Scratches her head and gets up unnecessarily. (Not sure about that one).

1889 Etiquette Quiz
- Is it allowable for a man to eat his meals with his coat off?
  Certainly not. No well-bred man would think of doing so.
  (That's gone out the window, too!)
- Is it proper to use a fork in eating asparagus, or should the stalks
  be taken in the fingers? Never use a knife. Well bred people take the stalks
  in their fingers. (Many are surprised to find out that that is still true!)

The placement of place cards >

The use and abuse of place cards is no trivial matter if you want the best experience at your event.

I attended a dinner party where place cards were on the dining table indicating where each guest should sit. Place cards are helpful for people to find their seats and they also add an elegant touch to a meal, formal or informal. One of the guests, unhappy with her place, removed her card and exchanged it for a more desirable (in her opinion) seat. She later complained that she didn't enjoy the evening because she wasn't included much in the conversation. Oh, my! This "lady" broke an etiquette rule and suffered the consequences.

The late Elsa Maxwell, who was internationally famous for her dinner parties, said "the most certain route to chaos at a dinner party is not having place cards telling everyone where to go." According to Letitia Baldridge, famous protocol advisor to the Kennedy Administration and currently a bestselling author on business protocol, "seating is a sensitive and logistically important aspect of good entertaining, whether one is giving a private party or a lunch for four hundred." It's a daunting job to seat a large party, especially when guests don't RSVP properly and drop on and off the list right up to the last moment. Anyone planning a wedding will immediately know what I mean!

This is where seating charts, door lists (for large events), and place cards come in. The savvy host will draw up a seating chart, make a door list (a list of guests names in alphabetical order, with a table number assigned to each person), and write place cards. Staff or caterers are supplied with the door lists and help the guests find their tables and seats.

It is a breach of etiquette to change a seating arrangement in the hope of making one's place better or more important. Hosts, whether at a private party or a corporate event, spend significant time on, and give considerable thought to, seating their guests. They have sound reasons for their decisions. There is precedent to consider; politics to consider; business alliances to consider. Additionally, the wise host will know who among the guests have little liking for one another – think of family holiday dinners!

Guests, then, should never change seats – no matter the reason. I refer you back to Letitia Baldridge who wrote, in *The Art of Business Entertaining*, "This kind of behavior can only be labeled as despicable." Strong words indeed!

So enjoy your next dinner party no matter where you are seated. You never know what friendship or business opportunity might develop.

ON BEING HOSPITABLE

The art
of hospitality >

The rules are less imposing
than in days of yore, but there is still
the responsibility to make guests
comfortable.

In ancient times, when traveling was dangerous, it was considered a sacred duty to welcome, cloth, feed, and shelter a visitor. The rules of hospitality were many and complicated.

English monarchs, whether to avoid plagues, or to stay in touch with their subjects and assert their sovereignty, made long journeys throughout their realms. Such an excursion was called a "royal progress." Queen Elizabeth I was legendary for her demanding ways as she compelled her courtiers to entertain her and her entourage on these royal meanderings. Often an aristocrat would be "chosen" for the honor of feeding and housing hundreds of ladies in waiting, servants, horses, dogs, grooms, and everything else connected with the royal progress.

Many of those unfortunate hosts went bankrupt as they struggled to maintain the standards of the monarch on stopovers that could last many weeks. Many a hostess suffered a nervous breakdown as she valiantly tried to cope with running what could be compared to a small city. Well, wouldn't we all.

Thankfully, today's hosts don't have such problems. When we invite guests into our homes, the rules of hospitality are simpler. Yet thoughtful hosts will make sincere efforts to welcome guests and see to their comfort. They will:

- Provide a welcoming bedroom, and the comfort of extra pillows.
- Provide lamps for reading.
- Leave several towels in the bedroom, along with fresh soap.
- Leave a little gift basket with goodies, including water.
- Leave plenty of lights on so guests can move easily and safely during the night.
- Empty some drawers, and leave closet space for personal belongings.
- Give information on attractions in the area, or take guests on a tour.
- Happily say, "Of course not, the housekeeper (that might be you) will do that," when guests ask if they should strip the bed.

The considerate guest, on the other hand, will:

- Bring a nice gift.
- Respect the household schedule.
- Take hosts for a meal if the visit lasts longer than one night.
- Participate enthusiastically in the host's plans.
- Criticize nothing.
- Not ask about stripping the bed, but just go ahead and do it, putting sheets, along with used towels in the pillow case, and placing the lot in or near the laundry.
- Write a nice thank you note.

Follow these simple steps and you will be the host everyone loves to visit, and the guest everyone loves to welcome into their homes.

A guide to good manners for the host and guest > (Part One)

Proper etiquette for a social event begins with managing the invitation and deciding what to wear.

Let's explore the duties and responsibilities of both the host(ess) and the guest. Remember, at a social event, whether for business or pleasure, the event is a two-way street. Both parties have a responsibility for its success – or failure.

The Invitation

We'll start with the invitation. There are several options here: a more formal printed invitation (not many can afford engraving these days); an email, e-vite or social media invitation (yes, these have become acceptable today); an invitation by phone or in person. The printed invitation, apart from giving the pertinent information – what, where, and what time – can also set the tone for the party. It will often give the recipient information on how to dress. This harkens back, by the way, to the court of Louis XIV, who had little etiquets (you'll note the word which was a precursor to etiquette) sent out to his court, telling people what to wear, where to stand, and how to behave.

The Response

The guest now has the responsibility to RSVP. This, again from the French, means répondez s'il vous plait, and that translates as "please reply" – whether or not you plan to attend. Note the word "not." A good guest will reply quickly to let the host(ess) know if he or she will attend or not.

Now what about bringing extra people? Oh, no, no, no, that is not your call! Assume that anyone not invited is… not invited. So, no children, pets, or houseguests. Now if you have houseguests, and relay that as the reason you can't attend, most hosts will welcome them. Be careful though, and listen to the language used. If the host says something like, "I have a full table, but maybe we could squeeze them in…"   best decline the invitation.

Dress Code

What about dress for the event? We all pretty much know what to wear for a formal occasion, such as a wedding, a black tie event, or even a business dinner. What about other events? When in doubt, just ask your host(ess). In my experience, it's better to overdress than underdress. After sizing up the other guest's attire, a man can always remove his tie, and roll up his sleeves. A woman can always remove excess jewelry.

So now the invitations have been issued and answered, and dress code is settled. Next we'll talk about how both the host and guest contribute to the event for maximum enjoyment for all.

A guide to good manners for the host and guest > (Part Two)

Proper etiquette for a social event
includes advanced preparation
by the host.

In Part One, we started a little "series" and talked about duties and responsibilities of both the host and the guest. We covered the invitation, the response, and the dress code. Now we'll talk about the savvy host. (Note: I'm going to say "host" from now on, with the understanding that I also mean "hostess.")

Advance planning is key to a successful event. Do as much as possible ahead of time, even if you are a seasoned host. Plan the menu, choose the wines, make lists, and shop early. A beautifully set table sets the tone for the evening, whether it be formal, informal, or a backyard barbecue. Guests become uneasy seeing a harried host rushing around setting the table, so do that ahead of time, too. Some of the nicest tables I have seen didn't have everything matching, so don't stress about that. Get creative, and use what you have in different and interesting ways. Fresh flowers always add a welcoming tone.

It's a good idea to know your guests' preferences and dietary restrictions. For instance, some religions prohibit pork and alcohol, so you wouldn't serve those items. Ask "is there anything you don't eat or drink," but don't worry too much about it after that; just make sure there are a few options.

Invite one or two tried and true guests that you know can carry on a good conversation, and can draw out the introverts. Use place cards (that's right, place cards!) if there are more than six people at a table. It prevents confusion about where to sit, and it allows the host to strategically place people. This becomes essential when planning important business meals.

If you are a gourmet cook, that's great! If not, remember it's not entirely about the food. Your guests will remember the warmth and hospitality of an event, long after the food. And should a guest be so lacking in manners so as to complain that the roast was tough, maybe you should consider not inviting him or her back!

The famous American chef Julia Childs said "A party without cake is really just a meeting." Do serve dessert – fresh fruit on a lovely platter; store bought or homemade goodies; gourmet cheeses with fruit – your guests can enjoy dessert with coffee, or even some well-chosen after dinner drinks.

So, the table is set; the wine is decanted; the food is (well, almost) prepared; the background music is good and not too loud.

It's time to welcome your guests. Showtime!

A guide to good manners for the host and guest > (Part Three)

Attendance at social events is about the contribution.

For the considerate guest:

- Please don't arrive early, as this will probably frazzle the hosts, and throw off their timing.
- If it's a dinner party, do let them know if you are going to be more than 15 minutes late.
- After you've greeted your host, it's time to move on and greet other guests.
- If you see someone standing alone, go over, put out your hand and introduce yourself. That's just a nice thing to do, and helps get the party started.
- Gifts: avoid arriving with an unarranged bouquet of flowers, forcing the host to vanish to find a vase.
- A flower arrangement or potted plant delivered by a florist early in the day, will delight the host!
- Be creative: don't always show up with the obligatory bottle of wine.
- Gourmet cookies and candies are always welcome, as are coffees, candles, or fancy soaps.
- Remember, it is the host's party, not yours.
- Author and culinary expert, Jeremiah Towers, said "Very little is about you at someone else's dinner party except your manners." So best bring those along.
- When seated, if there are place cards, do take your seat where you are designated to sit. Changing place cards is a very big "no-no!"
- If you have allergies or food aversions, now is not the time to tell your host, because you should have done that ahead of time.
- Now is the time to "sing for your supper" and be a charming and interesting guest.
- Truman Capote said "A conversation is a dialogue, not a monologue."
- Don't monopolize the conversation; let others shine too.
- Never criticize the food. Saying you don't like the food is childish.
- Burping: no matter what you've read or heard about how burping in some other cultures is fine and that a loud belch while dining is a compliment on the food...Well? Best not do that.
- Enjoy the wine, but not too much!
- Be aware of when it is time to leave.
- Say goodbye to the other guests, and tell them you enjoyed talking to them – even if you didn't! That's just good manners.
- Don't linger too long at the door when you say goodbye; and thank your host for an enjoyable evening. Remember to send a proper "thank you" note.
  Do all the above and you'll definitely be on the "A" list for the next party!

"Manners are a sensitive awareness of the feelings of others. If you have that awareness, you have good manners, no matter what fork you use."—Emily Post

Hostess on the hot seat >

Don't be surprised if you're surprised when hosting a party; it happens!

This is a cautionary tale. My husband and I recently gave a spur of the moment dinner party to say farewell to a bachelor friend who was leaving to take a position in another city. I asked him to let me know whom he would like to invite, even saying "as many as you like." After some texting back and forth, we had three couples, including my husband and me.

The day of the party arrived, and it was a blisteringly hot day, so I decided to prepare a cold meal. I happily set the table for six, and looked forward to a pleasant evening.
The guest of honor arrived first. Then another person arrived, whom I knew, but was not expecting. She was followed by a smiling couple that I had never seen before. To make a long story short, six guests became twelve!

What's a hostess to do? Well, here's what I did. I smiled and greeted, and greeted and smiled. I asked my husband to entertain the guests on the front covered porch. He served wine, lemonade and ice water, along with appetizers.

I grabbed a dear friend (one of the original six) who had been a caterer in another life, and asked (no begged!) him to come into the kitchen. While he plated the meal – very carefully, I might add – I set another table. I was grateful that I usually prepare lots of food, and thanks to my creative caterer friend, we had enough to make twelve attractive meals. Lots of ice cream and fresh fruit made a good dessert.

My husband kept the party going on the porch while all this was going on inside. I periodically popped out to cheerfully ask if anyone needed anything.

So what happened here? Frankly I don't really know. My friend must have taken my "as many as you like" comment to heart and invited the others. He just didn't tell me. But any fault lies with me. I should have checked with him personally (not by text!) to confirm the guest list.

So what does one do in a similar situation? Don't panic, and smile, smile, smile. Have plenty of libations; always make more food than you think you'll need, and pray that you have a trusted friend on hand to help.

Actually, despite the initial surprise, it was a lot of fun – and none of the other guests were any the wiser about the crisis in the kitchen. A wonderful evening was had by all – including yours truly!

OVER THERE

Clarifying the international lines of behavior >

On the world stage, a little patience goes a long way. So does homework.

Most of us are familiar with a favorite quote of the Chinese philosopher, Confucius, "All people are the same ...", but might not be familiar with the rest of the quote, "... It's only their habits that are different." Understanding that last part of the quotation is crucial to a successful international experience. The lines between countries and cultures are blurring, and savvy business people should do all they can to learn how to negotiate in the international arena.

Sometimes Americans think we can do business internationally in the same way we do it at home. That sort of thinking can get us into trouble and, without meaning to, we can end up offending the very people we want to impress. Americans are fast; we are linear in our thinking; we like to be on time; we want to get to the bottom line quickly and efficiently; in short, we want to get on with it.

That attitude usually doesn't work in a global setting. Patience is a great virtue when dealing in the international arena. When we are doing business abroad, we would do well to invest some time in increasing our cross cultural awareness. The study of differences between cultures takes years to master, so it stands to reason that Americans studying, working, or doing business abroad should devote substantial time and effort in an attempt to understand their host country, or the international visitor they are hosting here. It is important to learn a little of the subtleties and nuances of working in another culture.

While we Americans delight in being more casual in our own country, we need to be aware that the nuance of the social dance, which is the prerequisite to business in other cultures, is crucial to doing business successfully abroad. Here are some observations and tips that will help you appear polished and sophisticated:

- Most Americans are friendly and gregarious;
  we speak to everyone, even strangers.
- Some internationals, while admiring our ability
  to be informal and outgoing, may not be comfortable
  with instant friendliness. We can be perceived as brash
  and insincere.
- They usually know a great deal more about us
  and our ways than we know about them.
- Learn something of the geography, history and culture
  of your host country before you travel.
- Do not call your international colleague by her first name
  unless specifically asked to do so.
- Sometimes what appears to be a first name might be the last name.
  Do your homework.
- Casual introductions are not appreciated and can be construed as an insult.
- Rank and status are extremely important in other cultures.
- Internationals are often more formal and conservative in their manners and dress.
- And need I add, learn proper dining etiquette! You will be judged
  on your table manners.

Host for
international visitor >

Recognize the differences
between cultural expectations.

I served as host for international business colleagues visiting the United States for the first time. It was a pleasure for me to show them around, and watch them fall in love with this beautiful part of America.

Management guru Peter Drucker observed, "If you don't think globally, you deserve to be unemployed—and you will be." American professionals today realize that ethnocentricity—the concept that the world revolves around our culture—has no place in 21st century business relationships.

Roger Axtell, author of *Dos and Taboos of Hosting International Visitors*, notes that first time international visitors usually have four initial impressions. First: they are fascinated by the vastness of the United States and the huge distances we can travel. Secondly, they are struck by the many people who are overweight. They relate that to the abundant amount of food that is available everywhere. I won't comment here.

Another impression is the rapidity with which everything is done—how quickly Americans move, eat, and do business. The pace of American life is palpable; I always feel it when I returned from a trip abroad. The fourth impression is that we are outgoing and friendly to everyone. Those traits can sometimes land us in trouble with our more reserved international visitors. Here are some thoughts to consider as you prepare to host international colleagues:

- Observing rank and status is extremely important in other cultures.
- Friendliness should not cross the line when it comes to status and rank.
- Non-English speaking visitors are not deaf. Talking loudly will not improve their comprehension of English.
- When your visitor arrives, consider jet lag, and do not schedule events too soon after arrival.
- Be sensitive to dietary needs.
- Visitors from Arab countries might be offended if they are offered pork products.
- Some Chinese colleagues will be unable to eat the rare steak that Americans enjoy.
- Not all appetites (or tummies) can handle a heavy American breakfast.
- Plan a few outings around the history of your area.
- Shopping is a favorite with international visitors. No matter how sophisticated they appear, most love to spend time in an American shopping mall—yes, even the big box stores.
- Your visitor would be delighted to be invited into an American home.

Hosting international colleagues is rewarding. Call upon your American ingenuity, do a little research, and you will be amazed at the serendipitous things that will happen as a result.

The way we are >

It's nice to know how people overseas properly interact, but we need to know how we do it, as well.

I am sometimes asked by international colleagues to give them information on what to expect when they visit the U.S. on business. It struck me that we can learn a lot as professionals by remembering the advice we give to our visitors.

Handshaking: Modern etiquette says men and women shake hands in the U.S. and it doesn't matter who extends the hand first.

Eye contact: Amercians make direct eye contact.

Space: Americans have a greater need for space between people than in some other cultures, so try to keep at arm's length.

Hospitality: While Americans are friendly, outgoing and gregarious, they usually keep a small circle of close friends. A conundrum for our international friends is that, even if Americans welcome them warmly, they may not spend a great deal of time with them.

Clothes: It's fine to ask about the dress code for an event.

Parties: People usually introduce themselves at parties. Although you will see people sitting at gatherings, most people prefer to stand up and start moving around. When attending parties, make eye contact, smile and introduce yourself.

Smoking: Is a major no-no in the United States. If you smoke, do it outside and not in a doorway. As a guest in a home, never smoke in your bedroom with the door closed.

Perceptions: Americans value individual freedom and privacy. If a door is closed, knock and wait for a response.

English words: Can have multiple and different meanings.
For example:

- In America, we call them faucets, and you might call them taps.
- A dinner napkin is what some would call a serviette.
  A napkin is the word for diaper in England, Canada and New Zealand.
- What we call a "check" in a restaurant, you might call a "bill."

International issues: Newspapers in smaller communities do not carry much international news, so don't be surprised if we are not as knowledgeable as you about international issues. That doesn't mean we are not interested.

Note: As in other nations, criticism of our country is not welcome. Avoid giving your opinion on our system of government, our politics, religion, race relations, the wars in Iraq or Afghanistan, and other sensitive topics until friendships are more fully developed. Genuine interest is welcome, but avoid statements that can be perceived as judgmental.

Etiquette in the air >

A few simple courtesies
can make flying more pleasant
(and heaven knows, it needs to be).

A few years ago, there was a television series, set in the 1960s, called "Pan Am." It depicted glamorous "airline hostesses," fulfilling polite, well-dressed travelers' every request, and serving beautiful meals. The series didn't have high ratings, possibly because it all seemed so quaint and out of date. That's simply not our reality today.

Overcrowded airports and planes are straining to accommodate jam-packed passenger loads. Flight delays, rude passengers, small spaces and crying children add to the stress of modern flying. These conditions can strain even the most patient of travelers. This is where our automatic good manners take over. Showing courtesy and consideration often brings out the best in others, and can diffuse tense situations.

Some tips to consider for a successful flight:

- Always act in a courteous, respectful, articulate fashion.
- Dress well. Make no mistake about this: the better dressed you are
  the more respect you will receive.
- Avoid wearing sweat pants, and clothes that bare too much flesh.
- Show respect for the flight attendants. They have incredibly stressful jobs.
- Do not take up more space than your allocated seat or luggage compartment.
- Claiming one arm rest if fine, but taking both is inconsiderate and rude.
- When a child pushes or kicks your seat, stand up and smile,
  engage both the child and the accompanying adult, and ask him to stop.
- Bathroom line cutters: smile, say "Excuse me; the line is here."
  Point to the end of the line and say "thank you." If a child, escorted by an adult,
  needs to use the restroom, it might be wise to let him go ahead.
- Loud music, loud voices, bad jokes, foul language, or other rudeness:
  it's best to speak to the flight attendant. You might have to request another seat,
  hoping the flight is not booked completely. Smile and ask nicely.
- You specified a kosher or vegetarian meal and you didn't receive it.
  (This won't happen on domestic flights any more, unless you're travelling
  First Class.) Simply smile, ask for the correct meal, and if that doesn't work,
  remain gracious.
- Bringing garlicky or other strongly-spiced foods on board is offensive to others.
- The chatterer next to you wants to tell you the story of his life.
  After exchanging a few pleasantries, simply smile (is there a pattern here?)
  say excuse me "I need to sleep, read, or review my speech."

Bon Voyage!

The right gift around the world >

Don't give the Chinese clocks
or four of anything to a Korean.
And for heaven's sake, don't give
somebody from the Middle East
a handkerchief.

Let's talk about gift-giving in the professional world, especially in the international arena. Americans don't usually give business gifts, but many cultures view the ritual as a way of strengthening relationships. Americans can be overwhelmed by the generosity of international clients, and embarrassed that they have nothing to offer in return.

Be aware that many U.S. federal and state agencies either forbid gift-giving or have a strict limit on the cost. Some American corporations wish to avoid any hint of bribery. In other cultures, however, presenting gifts and the accompanying etiquette does have a key place in business dealings. That being said, gift giving can be fraught with peril. If you give presents to your international clients, make sure you know the appropriateness and the implication of your gifts.

Some tips:
- Always present a gift of high quality, and made in the U. S.
  (The latter is becoming increasingly difficult.)
- Make sure the present is light and portable. A bronze statue
  of one of our presidents is not a good idea here.
- Be sensitive about an appropriate time to present your gift.

Suggestions:
- Coffee table books about your region (just watch the weight).
- Something made regionally, like Jefferson cups from Virginia.
- Folding Binoculars.
- Quality photo frames.
- Key rings or money clips from top jewelers.
- If your client has a degree from an American university,
  items from the Alma Mater will be received with delight.

Gift taboos (and there are many more):
- Business gift giving is always reciprocated in China—
  not to reciprocate is bad manners.
- The time to present a gift in Japan is at the end of your visit.
- Don't give four of anything to a Japanese or Korean client.
  It's like our number 13.
- Don't give clocks to the Chinese—they're associated with funerals.
- Handkerchiefs, even beautiful lace or embroidered ones,
  are associated with tears in the Middle East.
- A Swiss Army knife would be welcome in some cultures, but not in others.
  It could signal the desire to cut off relationships.
- Flowers can contain land mines of unintended meanings, depending on the country.

So, do your homework and you will have another tool to maximize your potential in the international business world.

The concept of time >

We Americans are always in a hurry.
Not so much elsewhere.

Long before I started my etiquette and protocol business, I visited a Middle Eastern country on a business trip with my husband. It included appointments with the heads of universities, businesses and industries. We found that, although promptness was expected of us, we should be prepared to wait several minutes or even several hours to conduct our business. What?

I recall on one occasion being ushered into an enormous office where our host proved gracious and genial, offering refreshments, coffee, tea and fruit juice (it is rude to refuse such things in that culture), all the time making small talk. Others were in the room, and our host carried on several conversations at once, none of them relating to our agenda, although we were introduced and included. He talked on the telephone—even to his mother at one point. Although at the outset we were baffled and quite disturbed, we soon found that this was typical of the way business was conducted in Middle Eastern cultures.

Let's face it though, had we done just a little homework, we would have been prepared for what we encountered. You see, we were moving in a culture that views time differently than we view it. We were in a polychronic culture, where it is normal for several things to be happening at once. You get to the bottom line eventually, but a lot goes on between the greeting and signing the contract.

Americans operate on what is called monochronic time. We are fast, we do everything hurriedly, we value promptness, we are linear in our thinking, and we want to get to the bottom line quickly. In many international settings, this attitude can be counterproductive to our success. In fact, most of the rest of the world doesn't operate on our time lines.

A large percentage of newly-launched American businesses fail abroad because American business people don't study and learn the important subtleties and nuances of the host culture. Inflexible insistence on monochronic time frames at the very outset of new business dealings can determine whether or not relationships have a future

So, do your homework ahead of time. With a minimal knowledge of a different culture, you can come across as a savvy international professional. Believe me, you will find that wonderful, serendipitous things can and do happen if you are flexible and patient in your approach to doing business.

Traveling in France >

The advice: When in Rome…
applies to Paris, as well;
do as the Parisians do.

When I conduct seminars on international protocol I urge my clients to take the time to learn the culture of the country they are visiting. Understanding cultural differences can take years, so doing a little reading on the plane will not bring you up to speed as you deal with another culture – in either the business or social arena. I will be traveling abroad soon for business and pleasure. Paris is my first stop, and I am brushing up on my French and French culture.

The French consider themselves the arbiters of elegance and taste, and their demeanor can be rigid and formal. The word etiquette is French, and there are strict rules surrounding behavior and dress. While this is changing, "casual" behavior or dress is not appreciated.

Some consider the Parisians rude, but I have not found that to be my experience. Remembering the following will help you have a memorable time in the City of Light.

- The French are traditionalists. They revere their language,
  and insist that it be used properly.
- It is rude to start talking to a French person without a greeting:
  Bonjour Madame, Monsieur, or Mademoiselle, and acknowledging
  that your French is poor.
- Avoid the American impulse to rush up to a stranger and demand
  (in English) where the Metro or anything else is without first greeting
  the person in French. Then wait to be acknowledged. Most Parisians
  will respond to that courtesy, and help you out in English.
- The French don't usually smile at strangers. They are uncomfortable
  with joke telling, but love a good debate.
- Brush up on your French history, art and culture.
- The French are private people. Don't intrude on that privacy with queries
  about occupation, age, marital status, children, or health.
- Never inquire about political leanings—true in the U.S. also!
- Dress: the French consider themselves leaders of the fashion world.
  Dress is understated and elegant for both men and woman.
- Very casual clothes are not usually worn in cities.
- The French consider dining an art form, and much time is devoted
  to the discussion, ordering, and enjoying of both food and wine.
- It is a faux pas if you don't use a knife and fork properly!
- Tipping: gratuities are built into the cost of a meal, but you can round up,
  and add a little more if you like.

Perhaps I'll revisit this topic. It's been four years since I've been to France, and this is a rapidly changing world!

Three countries, three cultures >

This was written the day before
the tragic attacks in Paris; My heart
goes out to the beautiful people of
the City of Light.

Mark Twain said, "Travel is fatal to prejudice, bigotry, and narrow-mindedness, and many of our people need it sorely on these accounts. Broad, wholesome, charitable views of men and things cannot be acquired by vegetating in one little corner of the earth all one's lifetime."

I recently traveled to Paris, Florence, Rome and Istanbul. Three separate countries, and three separate cultures. We've all heard the caveats: "The French are lazy;" "The Italians are incompetent;" "All Muslims are terrorists." Those are examples of ethnocentrism and/or xenophobia. Ethnocentrism has been defined as "the belief that one's own culture is superior to all others and is the standard by which all other cultures should be measured." Xenophobia is "an unreasonable fear or dislike of foreigners or strangers, or of that which is foreign or strange."

Let me tell you my experience. In Paris, I noticed that the young woman behind the desk at our hotel, with whom my husband and I traded pleasant small talk before we went to dinner, was still there working the next morning. She told me it took her an hour and a half and two busses to get to work. The busboy who handled our luggage the first morning, was still working late into the night.

In Florence, we discovered we had forgotten a voucher for a tour of a Museum. Our hotel clerk went out of his way to contact our travel agent in the States, and obtain the voucher via email for us.

In Rome, we traversed the city by an "on and off bus." The driver navigated through streets that were filled with vehicles coming from all directions. Added to the chaos was the fact that the metro was on strike. We became concerned that we would be late for our appointment to tour the Vatican Museum, and voiced our concern to the driver. After thinking for a moment, he stopped his bus at a taxi stand, got out, hailed a taxi, and asked the driver to take us quickly to our destination.

In Istanbul, where I conducted four business etiquette seminars, our Muslim hosts made sure we had access to a Christian church on Sunday.

In the cities I visited I noticed a common theme: most people with whom I interacted worked long hours, often under stressful circumstances. Yet in these three countries with three distinct cultures there was a common theme of hard work and kindness. There's a lesson here for us all, don't you think?

Etiquette
in the airport >

For many of us who fly a lot,
it seems manners have been left far
behind, before arrival, for a number
of our fellow passengers.

In the last twelve months I have spent many hours in airports, traveling for both business and pleasure. Believe me, I have seen "the good, the bad, and the ugly" when it comes to human behavior in airports!

During the holiday seasons, hundreds of thousands of us will travel by air to celebrate with family and friends. Earlier, I talked about civility while flying on the plane. Now let's talk about behavior in the airport, going through security, boarding the plane, taking one's seat, and deplaning.

An airport can be an abysmal place to be during the holidays, and things can become frustrating. Flights get overbooked, delayed, or cancelled. Let's face it, there is really nothing one can do about it except to understand that the airline's staff is doing its best to accommodate passengers. Here is the time to remember that a little grace and good manners can go a long way.

Savvy travelers:

- Make sure they have an app on their smart phone to rebook a flight fast if theirs is cancelled.
- Dress well—oh, yes, it makes a difference in the way you're treated!
- Arrive early.
- Respect the carts that are ferrying passengers. Are aware of the beep warning of an approach, and avoids walking in front of them.
- Are prepared for security by having the boarding pass and I.D, in hand.
- If not TSA Pre-checked, are ready to remove coats, shoes, belts, have the computer ready to take out, along with liquids stored in a clear, plastic, zip-top bag.
- Are courteous to the screening employees, complies with their instructions, and thanks them.
- Once through security—move away from the conveyor belt! Take possessions to a bench or table to get out of people's way for reassembly, which keeps the lines moving.
- Respect the carryon luggage rules. If wearing a back pack, don't whack others while turning around. Not nice!
- Wait patiently at the gate until their group is called, without bucking the line. That causes anger, and that in turn causes bad behavior.
- If seated on the aisle, wait until fellow row passengers are seated before buckling your seat belt.
- Respect the flight attendants, and the job they do.
- Wait their turn to deplane.
- Allow those with a tight connection to deplane first.

Air travel can be frustrating and exhausting. Acting out, complaining and griping never helps. The next time you fly, take the high road, and bring your good manners along!

A diplomatic dilemma >

How do we best bridge the gap
between the demanding guest and the
unaccommodating host... whether on
the international front or your own
business front?

In January 2016, Iranian President Hassan Rouhani made the first state visit to Europe by an Iranian president in almost two decades. The purpose of the trip, which was highly anticipated in Europe, was to rebuild economic ties following the lifting of sanctions against Iran.

In France a diplomatic squabble occurred that involved luncheon plans for the French President François Hollande and President Rouhani The dispute centered around the Iranians insistence on an alcohol-free meal with halal meat. Halal is Arabic for "lawful" or "permitted" and is used to designate how meat is treated.

Well! One report said, "This amounted to culinary sacrilege in France." French officials insisted on serving traditional food and wine, saying making a meal "Iran friendly" went against their values. Luncheon was cancelled. As an alternative, alcohol free breakfast was suggested. That was vetoed as being too "cheap." The presidents reportedly settled for a perfunctory face-to-face meeting.

That meeting was hardly comparable to what happened in Italy, where the meeting went seamlessly. In Rome, Rouhani met with Italian Prime Minister Matteo Renzi, Pope Francis, and various Italian companies. Alcohol was nowhere in sight, and officials even covered up the ancient nude statues! The two countries signed deals reportedly worth billions of dollars.

It's unlikely that most of us will encounter the sort of international diplomatic impasse that occurred in Paris. So let's bring the matter closer to home, because similar situations do occur in our business and social lives. How would you balance the following?

- The host should always accommodate a guest.
- A guest should not place demands on the host.
- When in Rome, do as the Romans do—so adapt to the situation.
- The client is always right.
- One should never abandon one's principles.

All of the above are correct, of course. However, wars have erupted between countries, business colleagues, and families through a lack of diplomacy, business protocol, or just plain good manners.

Etiquette dictates that:
- A host does everything possible to accommodate a guest's likes and dislikes.
- A guest should let the host know of any dietary restrictions or allergies.
- A guest should not dictate what a host serves, any more than he/she
  should dictate the guest list.

Clearly, diplomacy is more than just polite conversation in elaborate settings. It involves a careful, delicate balancing act, and hard decisions. As author Christopher Nutall said: "Diplomacy is the art of getting what you want without offending anyone too badly." Excellent observation in today's "prickly" world!

American and European styles of eating >

How you handled your utensils used to identify from which side of the pond you resided.

I conducted an etiquette dinner for a well-known university that had a highly successful football program. Imagine me, all five feet of me, trying to instruct these huge young men, looking down at me from an enormous height (and who were not the least bit interested), on proper dining skills! Knowing that most of these young athletes would go on to some sort of professional career, either playing or coaching, I challenged them with the notion that, if successful, they would attend a lot of banquets. Asking them if they felt comfortable using the silverware and glasses that were laid out in front of them, most admitted that they did not. Ah, the teachable moment!

The conversation led to the differences between the American style and the European or Continental styles of eating. A little history: until the 1840's Europeans and Americans ate in the same style, knife set on the right, fork on the left, laying the knife down on the side of the plate after cutting the meat, and moving the fork to the right hand. Then the English stopped shifting their forks back and forth, and began eating with the fork in the left hand and the knife in the right. In 1853 the French decided that the English way was correct, and before long all of Europe was eating in the English style. Not the independent Americans, though! They stayed with the original method and style of eating.

The athletes were fascinated to learn that, during WWII, American spies in Germany, often blew their cover by the way they handled a knife and fork. You will sometimes see that in old WWII movies. American spies might have spoken the language perfectly, had an excellent grasp of the culture and customs, but they betrayed themselves by eating in the American style.

Some etiquette books insist that one must eat like an American in America, and use the Continental method when in Europe. This is a complete fallacy. In today's world, whether it be business or social, using both styles is correct, no matter which side of the pond you are on. Using a combination of both is also correct.

The student/athletes enjoyed learning how to eat in the European or Continental style. In fact, some of them preferred the latter style, saying it was more practical and more efficient, since it skipped a step. Try it at your next dinner party—but practice first!

Socializing
in Ireland >

A visit to Ireland by Americans
is a pleasurable experience (for both
parties); here are some social
graces to keep in mind.

The 1990s up to the late 2000s there was an economic explosion in the Republic of Ireland, as American technology companies invested heavily in the country. The result was rapid economic growth, with its attendant jobs, and this was called the "Celtic Tiger." Although the rapid growth did not last, Ireland is still a grand place to do business, and of course, to socialize.

I was born in Ireland and I am often asked about my country. Here are a few observations that you might enjoy as you explore "the land of Saints and Scholars." The Irish people are genuinely friendly and welcoming; nevertheless you might want to be aware of some refinements that would make visiting this beautiful land even more enjoyable.

- The ancient language is called Irish and not Gaelic. There has been a resurgence of the Irish language in the last few decades, and you will find that all official guides will greet you in both Irish and English.
- Try not to fake the Irish accent – never works – embarrassing, really.
- Please don't say "Top o' the mornin' to ya!" Irish people don't use this phrase at all, and you may be laughed at if you do.
- The social hub in any town or village is the pub. To participate in the experience, buy your round of drinks for everyone in your party. You'll be considered rude if you don't. By the way, it doesn't need to be Guinness!
- While drinking alcohol is part of the Irish culture, there are serious consequences if you are caught drinking and driving.
- The Irish language has no equivalent of "Yes" and "No." This has translated down through the centuries to the English language, so it may sound strange to visitors when they don't receive a direct answer to a question. Listen carefully to the syntax though, and you will be charmed!
- Most Irish people are great conversationalists. They love the spoken word, and most use it brilliantly. It can be a joy to hear them playing with the language.
- Religion and politics are definitely off limits. These subjects can be very sensitive, so, as in any other country, best steer clear of them.
- Make sure you get into a conversation with the taxi drivers. They will give an opinion and advice on practically anything. I fondly remember a conversation with a driver in Dublin. He gave an eloquent, and extremely funny, interpretation of an art exhibit in the Museum we had just visited, opening with the observation, "I didn't like the way it (the art) was hung."
- The Irish love Americans. They also love good conversation, a well told story, poems, and song. So, as the party continues, don't be shy about showing your talent. You'll be welcomed Cead Mile Failte – a hundred thousand times! Slainte! (pronounced *SLAWN*-cha) To your Health!

SPECIAL MOMENTS

Family holidays >

Here's how to take the tension out of family holidays.

Each holiday season we are bombarded by commercials and movie specials that feature perfect families with beautiful manners, having a wonderful time. Of course, this is not reality, and some holiday gatherings end up in disaster. It occurred to me that that large extended family which I entertain during the Holidays is the prototypical American family: four generations including toddlers, children, teenagers, blended families, vegetarians, different religions, different politics and different traditions. Dare I drop a stray international business associate into this complicated mix?

Family holidays are wonderful but they can also be filled with tension. Every year some hosts work frenetically to satisfy their own and others expectations. Each person brings memories from past holidays, the joy or pain of previous years and sometimes unrealistic expectations.

Here's where our automatic good manners should take over, because good manners pull us through the rough patches. Good manners also keep us from saying or doing things we might regret later.

The Hosts

- Take a deep breath, and realize this is not a Formal State Occasion.
- Remember what makes a holiday gathering special is not "things."
  It's the time spent together and memories made.
- Don't think you need to do everything yourself. Accept help.
- When you encounter real or implied criticism, smile, and carry on.
- Seat potential antagonists at opposite ends of the table, or better yet, at another table.
- Have a children's table, and make it special.
- Arrange for adults (the fun adults) to take turns supervising the children.
- Have activities for children after dinner.
- Remember those loved ones who are no longer with us.
- In our family, around desert time, my husband gives a little update on each person.
  This is oral history being passed on to younger generations.

The Guests

- Arrive anticipating a wonderful time.
- Try not to criticize anybody or anything.
- Participate fully.
- Be part of the solution, not the problem.
- If you have children, please keep an eye on them yourself!
- Genuinely express your appreciation.

Holiday parties:
A time to behave >

Keep in mind that the annual
holiday event is a business function,
and an extension of the work day.

The holiday season is a season of good cheer, and good feelings towards others. The corporate world usually spends time and money on holiday parties to promote their businesses, and thank their employees and clients. These events are wonderful opportunities to advance your career or business. They are also nice opportunities to meet high level executives or clients with whom you would normally not interact. Smart professionals will use this to their advantage.

These occasions are also wonderful opportunities to ruin your reputation! We've all heard about the people who over-served themselves with alcohol, told off the boss, or passed out (horror!) at the table. Keep in mind that the annual holiday event is a business function, and an extension of the work day. It may be wrapped around a celebration of the season, but it is still a business event. It is always more "business" than "party."

- Don't ignore the invitation: your absence will be noted.
- Do be sure you know exactly who is invited to the party.
  Spouses or partners might not be included on the guest list
  for business events.
- Do inquire about the dress code.
- Do realize that the business holiday party is a business event,
  so conservative party clothes are a good choice.
- Don't wear anything too revealing or too flashy.
- Do make sure you greet your host(s).
- Do stay for at least 30 minutes.
- Do act professionally at all times.
- Don't drink too much.
- Don't use this occasion to let your hair down.
- Do keep your right hand free so that you can shake hands.
- Do keep your drink in your left hand, so you are not offering
  a cold wet handshake.
- Do mingle and introduce yourself to someone you don't know.
- Don't spend all evening talking business, or monopolizing the host.
- Don't overstay your welcome.
- Don't forget to thank the persons who planned
  and coordinated the party—often a thankless task.
- Do say goodbye to your host(s) – it is bad form to sneak away!
- Offer to be the designated driver and, need I say it,
  don't drink and drive!

All that said, decide ahead of time that you are going to enjoy this occasion—since it's important that you attend anyway. And the smart professional always sends a thank you note to the person hosting the party! Happy Holidays!

Protocol, pomp and circumstance >

The business meaning of "protocol" is an important distinction.

The marriage of Prince William to Ms. Catherine Middleton dazzled two billion people including many on this side of the pond. Since Prince William is not yet the heir apparent to the throne (that's his father, Prince Charles) the wedding was not a full state occasion. Nevertheless, it was full of pomp, pageantry and protocol. No doubts about it, the British know how to do that. We can put on a good show in this country, too. Think of the Presidential Inaugurations and Presidential funerals you have watched on television. Like the Royal wedding, these events are full of pageantry and the protocol of these occasions is planned out to the last detail.

The word "protocol" comes from two Greek words protos meaning the first and kola, meaning glue. They refer to an official document glued to a paper, thus giving it authenticity. Sort of like our Notary Public seal. Protocol is a prescribed set of procedures detailing rules for official documents and ceremonies that involve governments and their representatives. Whenever there are heads of state present, proper protocol is crucial. Wars have been started because of a real or perceived lack of protocol.

In business today, we often use the word protocol instead of etiquette because it sounds more businesslike. Its meaning is actually the more formal of the two words, but it sounds less stuffy.

We have other ceremonies that are full of pomp and protocol. Commencements in colleges and universities uphold a tradition that goes back to the famous medieval universities of Paris and Bologna. In medieval times people wore flowing robes, with materials and colors representing wealth, rank, professions and trades. Those dazzling robes are the ancestors of the gowns worn in academia today. Part of the thrill of a commencement is when the president, trustees, administration, faculty and degree candidates process in their colorful academic regalia to stirring music.

Each color on the hood signifies an academic discipline.
Some examples:
- Blue-violet, architecture
- Crimson, communication or Journalism
- Light blue, education
- White, English
- Orange, engineering
- Apricot, nursing
- Dark Blue, philosophy or political science
- Scarlet, theology

The Duke and Duchess of Cambridge will undoubtedly visit the U.S. in the future. When that happens, we'll pull out all the bells and whistles. And it would be a faux pas to address Prince William's bride as Kate or Princess Catherine. She is Catherine, Duchess of Cambridge. Why? That's the protocol.

A toast to you >

Here are a few basics—and
a little history—to make your
next toast a memorable one.

The beginning of the year rang in with cheerful toasts of "Happy New Year!" Like many customs, the history of "toasting" goes back to ancient times, perhaps to the Greeks, when it was not uncommon to poison one's enemy. The host would drink the mead or wine first, thus reassuring his guests of his lack of hostility.

Then there is the theory that a piece of toast was placed in the bottom of a goblet, and when "Toast!" was shouted, one had to drain the vessel quickly right down to the toast. This strange custom is rarely, if ever, practiced today, and certainly one would never entirely drain a glass!

Business dinners are occasions that call for a toast. Whether the toaster or the toasted, the smart professional will learn the basics in order to offer or receive a toast with poise and assurance. A good toast is short, often — but not always — funny, and is spoken from the heart. It appears spontaneous, but unless you are a talented extemporaneous speaker, better be well prepared and well-practiced. The right toast greatly adds to an occasion, and one that is well prepared, and delivered, can be remembered long after the event has past. Yet we can all recall occasions when the toast was too rushed, too long, embarrassing, just plain awkward, or (horrors!) written out and read.

The rules for toasting, whether in a professional or social setting, are simple:

- It is rude and disrespectful to refuse to participate in a toast.
  Refusing to raise your glass to toast is considered very impolite.
- Although wine and champagne are the usual libations,
  today it is perfectly acceptable to toast with water.
- Inverting one's glass is not done in polite society.
- If you are a guest do not make a toast until the host does.
- The first toast is made by the host who stands and welcomes the guests.
- When desert is served, the host stands and toasts the guest of honor.
- Do not tap the glass with the silverware to get attention — not good form.
- Do not say "I'm not a very good speaker."
  That will become obvious if it's true – best not advertise the fact!
- Clinking of glasses is permitted. Be careful though when fine crystal is used: hosts can lose their genial demeanor if the antique crystal is shattered!
- The guest receiving the toast remains seated, and does not drink to the toast.
  That would be akin to honoring oneself, and that is very bad form.
- Later it is appropriate for the guest of honor to stand and thank those
  who have honored him or her, and may or may not offer a toast in return.

Health, happiness and prosperity in the New Year!

Public performance protocol >

When you're out and about,
here's how to behave.

Let's talk about the movies, concerts, opera, and the theatre. Each has a slightly different code of behavior.

Classical Music Concerts:
- Dress code has relaxed in recent times, but please don't wear shorts and flip flops.
- Arrive early, and take your seat well ahead of the concert: Late arrivals are expected to wait until the usher directs you to your seat. Slightly embarrassing this.
- Greet the conductor's entrance with applause.
- Silence during a performance is a must. Coughing, wiggling about, rustling with cough drops will result in glares and a tsk tsk or two.
- Do not applaud between movements—it's bad form at classical concerts.
- When in doubt wait until the entire audience applauds.
- Shouting encore at the end of a performance is welcomed. Most groups already have an encore planned.

Opera:
- There's no need to wear your tails and tiaras, but dress appropriately for the occasion.
- It is acceptable, indeed expected, to applaud enthusiastically during a well-known aria, even if the music continues.
- Shouting bravo! (great!) for the male, and brava! for the female, or even bravissimo! for a particularly stirring performance is welcomed. I'd reserve that fine distinction, however, for the more experienced opera goer.
- Children: be careful here... opera lovers do not tolerate fussy children.

Live Theatre:
- You will have to wait to be seated if the performance has started.
- Sit in your assigned seat.
- Don't leave your seat until intermission.
- It is dangerous to the performers to use flash photography.
- In musical theatre, the overture is a part of the performance, so please stop talking.
- Lovebirds, when you lean your heads together, the people behind you can't see.
- Children are expected to be quiet and stay in their own seats.
- Leaving while the show is in progress and before the final curtain call is discourteous.

Movies:
- Purchase your snack(s) ahead of time.
- Pick up your trash.
- Don't put your feet on the seat in front of you.

Rock Concerts:
- Behavior here is less restrictive, but don't leave your manners behind.
- Standing, clapping, dancing, singing,and waving lit cell phones are part of the experience.
- Throwing something on stage might get you escorted out by a guard.
- Similarly, attempting to get on stage will make the guards nervous, and out you go.

I know I don't need to remind most of you, but do turn off your cell phones. Except for rock concerts, where they won't be heard anyway.

Protocol – does it really matter? >

Think protocol has no place
in your business or entertaining life?
It's time to think again.

I am often asked about the difference between etiquette and protocol, and why they matter anyway. There are many, and complicated, definitions of both words, but let's make it simple. Etiquette or manners is how we behave towards others in our professional and social lives. I like to think of protocol (the word comes from the Greek) as etiquette plus. In addition to the rules of behavior towards others, protocol adds a rather complicated layer of rules and instructions that govern international relations and diplomacy.

Some think this sort of thing is totally irrelevant today. They believe that, in an equal society, giving people rank, fussing over proper seating for diplomats, or making sure the military are addressed properly, is a bunch of... well, you fill in the word! Many simply don't "get" that it is crucial for those in military, diplomatic, and official life to be accorded their rank. They need to know what to do, when to do it, when to stand up, when to sit, who is introduced first, the list is endless. Knowing demonstrates good manners, eliminates confusion, and guarantees that an occasion will go seamlessly.

Think of Presidential inaugurations you've witnessed, or state funerals of former Presidents. How do they proceed so flawlessly? You can bet that there is more than one protocol officer behind the scenes directing the entire complicated event. And by the way, rehearsals for these events sometimes have taken place for months, even years.

In the business world you might not have to deal with precedence. However, if you are in charge of a business dinner, better be aware that many high powered executives have large egos. Seat them at different tables, and in that way no egos are bruised. Assign a host to each table, and place the most important woman and man to the right and left of the host. This treats them as guests of honor. Remember the most important person sits at the right of the host(ess).

It is up to the host(ess) to introduce himself or herself and the guests of honor, and set the tone for the evening. The host who doesn't do that sets the wrong mood for the occasion. Instead of lively, engaging conversation, the atmosphere can become stiff and uncomfortable. Remember, before an agreement is signed, the important decisions have usually been made around the dinner table

Protocol does matter – even in these casual times. You just might find that you need it more often than you think!

Holiday office parties and gifts >

If you work for a religious organization you probably know what's acceptable. But if you don't, here's some practical advice.

Office holiday parties and gift giving customs have changed in the past few decades. Years ago, the typical Christmas party in the corporate world was for employees only. No spouses invited, thank you! Lots of alcohol and high jinks were not uncommon, and really not frowned upon. Not so today. We are sensitive to the fact that not everyone celebrates Christmas. We usually (or should) include spouses or guests of employees, and heavy alcohol consumption at office parties is definitely out.

What about a Christmas tree, or would this offend non-Christians? What about gifts? Is it appropriate to give gifts to your boss, your boss's boss, your peers, your subordinates? And if you do that, what kind of hit will that take on your budget? What kind of gifts are appropriate? In the past a good bottle of wine or liquor did the trick, but check out the culture of your company before trying that now. In fact it would be a good idea to find out company policy about office parties and appropriate gifts before you start planning.

Some professionals opt for an office luncheon, and let it go at that. Some offices elect to do a White Elephant party, and I've seen some hilarious times associated with that. If your office decides on that, just make sure there are some guidelines for gifts. Be creative, and give a real white elephant that is fun, but not risqué.

What about the office curmudgeon or introvert who simply doesn't want to be bothered with all this? Or the person of another religion where Christmas is not celebrated? I have a Jewish friend who is very uncomfortable with anything associated with Christmas, and another who thoroughly enjoys it. I also have a Moslem friend who is delighted by the customs, from selecting the Christmas tree, to going to Christmas services, to cooking the Christmas dinner.

So what's really going on here? I think the etiquette surrounding these events is subject to the culture of your particular office environment. So do a little homework and find out what works for your particular group before you pull out the decorations.

Remember the purpose of these holiday gatherings and gift exchanges is to make people feel included. These are opportunities to get to know and bond with our colleagues. This in a season where the world feels a little kinder and, in this writer's opinion, there is goodwill towards men... and women!

Bridal showers
(a brief history) >

They've changed over the years,
but they remain an integral part
of many weddings.

Summer is traditionally the most popular time for weddings, and before the wedding comes the bridal shower. Although the bridal shower has its roots in the dowry, an ancient practice whereby money, goods, or lands were brought into the marriage by the bride, it is not the same thing at all.

Today's bridal showers come in all forms and would be hardly recognizable by the bride of the 1890s when the tradition in the U.S. was borne among the upper classes. The bridal shower was originally a spontaneous, informal gathering. Friends arrived without warning and brought gifts. The name "shower" might have arisen from the custom of putting the gifts in a parasol (a fancy umbrella) which when opened, showered the bride with presents. By the 1930s the custom was widespread in the United States. Showers were usually held about a month before the wedding, in the afternoon (remember ladies usually didn't work outside the home) or in the evening.

By the middle of the 20th century, planning guides and advice on special themes and games flourished. One thing remained unchanged, though: the shower was given by women for women. In the past, most showers outfitted the kitchen and the bedroom. This was probably because women were traditionally cooks, homemakers and, well, you know the rest. It was not good form for mothers, sisters or close family members to hold the bridal shower. It was considered offensive, even greedy, for family to solicit gifts for family. That custom has also changed over the decades, although this writer agrees with the convention.

Today, the bridal shower may take many different forms, and it is really up to the hostess and the bride to decide the theme. Some showers go completely over the top, with huge meals at fancy country clubs, and expensive presents. Others retain the more simple tradition of good friends getting together, bringing simple presents, and honoring the bride.

- Showers traditionally do not have the formal etiquette like that of a wedding.
- Bridesmaids or close friends usually are hosts.
- The purpose is gift-giving, so everyone is expected to bring a present.
- Invitations can be issued informally, by mail, email, e-vite or telephone.
- Themed showers are popular, e.g. linen showers, gourmet cookware, or even lingerie showers.
- Couples showers have become popular, and men now are often included in the festivities.

A happy thought: If you are invited to the shower, you can expect an invitation to the wedding.

Wedding guest etiquette >

Wedding behavior requires proper attention: yes it's that important.

I appeared on a local television talk show to discuss "do's and don'ts for wedding guests." May through August are the most popular months for weddings in most of the country, with June being the traditional time to tie the knot.

There is a plethora of etiquette advice for the bride, groom and families. What about advice for the wedding guests? Here is a short list of do's and don'ts that, as guests, we should follow.

Do's:

- Do, please, RSVP! That means "répondez s'il vous plait" in French, and "respond if you please" in English. Guests not responding are probably the most distressing part of wedding planning. RSVP means respond whether or not you plan to attend. So do respond as quickly as possible. It is just good manners to do so.
- Do dress appropriately. A beach wedding requires different dress than does a formal evening wedding.
- Do arrive for the ceremony in plenty of time
- Do sit at your assigned table—its plain tacky to change place cards!
- Do respect the couple's religious traditions.
- Do rest assured if you are married, engaged, or have a partner, that the invitation should include your guest.

Don'ts:

- Don't show up with an uninvited guest—that includes your children.
- Please don't ask to add a guest.
  It is simply not ok, and puts the bride in an awkward position.
- Don't dress to compete.
- Need I say it? Please don't wear white
- Don't text, tweet, email or Instagram.
  Your job is to enjoy the celebration, not report it.
- Don't upstage the couple by sending out photos before they do.
  Hurt feelings result in that!
- Don't leave before the cake is cut.

Wedding gifts: There is a lot of conflicting advice on this! This writer agrees with Miss Manners when she says "...a wedding invitation does not constitute an invoice." You give a present because you want to wish the happy couple well, not because you are obliged to do so. Nor are you obliged to use a wedding registry. Oh, I know I'm stepping on toes here! A wedding gift should be a thoughtful, loving gesture that reflects the giver.

Finally, do be a great guest. Introduce yourself to both sets of families. It helps to break the ice. And do help make the occasion a success by participating and enjoying the celebration!

New Year's resolutions >

A new year is a perfect time
to consider character improvement.

Well, we've rung in the New Year with some sort of libation – lively or not – and most of us made New Year's resolutions. This tradition dates back (as traditions usually do) to the Babylonians and Romans. Ancient Babylonians promised their gods each year that they would return borrowed objects and pay their debts. The Romans started the year by making promises to the God, Janus, after whom the month is named. In Medieval times, knights re-affirmed their chivalry by taking the "peacock vow" during the final feast of Christmas. Each would place their hand on a peacock (roasted or live) and re-dedicate themselves to the principles of chivalry for the coming year.

There are other religious equivalents to this tradition. During Rosh Hashanah and ending in Yom Kippur (Day of Atonement), Jews meditate on their transgressions of the past year, asking for forgiveness. Some Catholics fast during Lent, and in fact this writer as a little girl, used to give up candy for Lent. So the concept is fairly universal. But regardless of religion, it has to do with annual reflection and promises of self-improvement.

When Benjamin Franklin was twenty, he developed a method to improve his character. These were his thirteen virtues. Here they are, with the original grammar and spelling intact:

1. **Temperance.** Eat not to dullness; drink not to elevation.
2. **Silence.** Speak not but what may benefit others or yourself;
   avoid trifling conversation.
3. **Order.** Let all your things have their places;
   let each part of your business have its time.
4. **Resolution.** Resolve to perform what you ought;
   perform without fail what you resolve.
5. **Frugality.** Make no expense but to do good to others or yourself;
   i.e., waste nothing.
6. **Industry.** Lose no time; be always employ'd in something useful;
   cut off all unnecessary actions.
7. **Sincerity.** Use no hurtful deceit; think innocently and justly,
   and, if you speak, speak accordingly.
8. **Justice.** Wrong none by doing injuries, or omitting the benefits that are your duty.
9. **Moderation.** Avoid extremes; forbear resenting injuries so much
   as you think they deserve.
10. **Cleanliness.** Tolerate no uncleanliness in body, cloaths, or habitation.
11. **Tranquillity.** Be not disturbed at trifles, or at accidents common or unavoidable.
12. **Chastity.** Rarely use venery but for health or offspring, never to dullness,
    weakness, or the injury of your own or another's peace or reputation.
13. **Humility.** Imitate Jesus and Socrates.

Good luck with your resolutions, and Happy New Year!

St. Valentine's Day etiquette >

Celebrating Valentine's in
a personal—or business environment:
there's a difference.

It is generally agreed that the tradition of St. Valentine's Day goes back to the ancient Roman festival of Lupercalia, a fertility festival. Pope Gelasius, around the fifth century, decreed February 14 to be St. Valentine's Day, and the 14th century poet, Chaucer, linked love and St. Valentine's Day.

The tradition grew each century, and by the 18th century exchanging gifts and beautiful handmade cards were popular in England. These cards were made of lace and ribbons, with cherubs, cupids and hearts abounding. The tradition spread to America, and in the mid 1850's Esther Howland of Worcester, Massachusetts started to mass produce cards. In the ensuing decades the holiday evolved into what is now a huge commercial venture. Hundreds of millions of cards, along with flowers and chocolate will be sent or given this St. Valentine's Day.

Let's talk about Valentine's Day in the professional setting. If you are planning to send your greetings to the office, consider the following:

- Will the object of your affections (male or female) feel comfortable getting a huge bouquet of flowers at work?
- Some workplaces have rules in place about accepting gifts from clients or professional associates. Check to ensure that it's all right to send a gift.
- Don't send a smoking hot e-card ! Some companies monitor emails, and you could end up embarrassing your heart's delight.
- Nix the personal gifts for the office: jewelry, perfume, and lingerie are best given in a private setting.
- Don't try to impress your boss with a gift. It could be construed as toadying.
- If you plan to give a co-worker a Valentine's card, make sure it's appropriate, friendly or funny.
- If you send a funny card to a colleague, make sure he or she enjoys and understands your sense of humor.

So enjoy Valentine's Day and keep it light and professional in an office setting. If you send a box of chocolates, make sure it is big enough for your valentine to share with co-workers. If you send flowers or balloons, do include a card!

Finally, and for those who work in an office: remember when you were in grade school there was always someone who never received a Valentine's card? Be kind, look around and see the person who always seems to be on the outside of things. Send that person a friendly card. You might say "thank you for all you do!" You could make that person's day a little brighter!

Wedding guests >

Recognizing the guests in one's celebration enhances the occasion and results in a more memorable experience.

The date is set, the invitations are perfect, the wedding and reception venues are spectacular, the dress is drop dead gorgeous, the bridesmaids are beautiful, the groom and the groomsmen are handsome, the officiator is set, and plans are complete for your special day. What are we missing? Well, maybe the guests.

It has been said that weddings today have become entirely about the bride and groom. This writer, who has attended and/or directed hundreds of weddings, would like to offer some observations to the starry-eyed couple (and their parents!).

Consider this. Your nearest and dearest will be assembled, all at once, to celebrate and support you as you start your life together. Some will have traveled great distances (perhaps at great expense) to share in your special day. Think about ways to make them feel cherished, welcomed, and appreciated. Make it less about you, and more about them, and your wedding will be a beautiful memory for everyone.

I will never forget a wedding and reception to which my husband and I were invited in Istanbul. And it wasn't the lavish wedding, held in an incredible old palace in the ancient city, overlooking the Bosporus that made the occasion so memorable. What sticks in my memory was the genuine hospitality shown by the bride and groom and their families. In that culture, a guest is always welcomed and shown unfailing courtesy.

The bride and groom visited every table, taking time to talk and pose for photographs with each guest. This replaced the receiving line, which, when there are lots of guests, can really hold up things. What a gift! This young couple showed us how much they appreciated our presence.

Be thoughtful, and anticipate your guests comfort:

- Place a welcome basket in their hotel rooms. Nothing elaborate—
  maybe water, fruit, nuts, and cookies. It says "welcome, so glad you're here!"
- Invite all out of town guests to the rehearsal dinner. This is considered mandatory.
- Go over your seating in the church with the ushers. Use a chart.
- Make sure that close relatives are seated properly.
- Try not to hold up the reception with "just one more photograph."
- A cash bar? Oh my. Very bad form!
- Vary the music at the reception so that all ages can enjoy it.
- Do make sure you send a warm, timely "thank you" note
  acknowledging wedding presents.

Now relish your day, knowing you have done your best to include everyone in the occasion!

Flag etiquette >

Treatment of the flag should be done with respect, regardless the level of patriotism.

When my youngest son was a very little boy he looked forward with great anticipation to visiting his grandfather. Each morning and evening they raised and lowered the American flag together. I can still see this little boy lowering the flag, while the elderly gentleman admonished "don't ever let the American flag touch the ground." That little boy grew up to be a career officer in the United States Marine Corps. I have often thought that the seeds of his patriotism were sown during those long ago days with his grandfather.

Some Americans think that patriotism and showing respect for the American flag is not "cool." As we prepare to celebrate Independence Day, let's reflect for a moment on respect for our flag. In 1942, Congress passed a joint resolution which was to become Public Law 829 "The Flag Code." This code definitively states the correct use and display of the flag for all occasions. Most of us have a working knowledge of the "do's of flag etiquette. Let's look at the Code to see specific instructions on how you don't use the flag.

They include:

- The flag should never be dipped to any person or thing.
- The flag should never be displayed upside down, except to signal distress in instances of extreme danger to life or property.
- The flag should never be used as drapery or any decoration. (I remember a friend of mine, a paragon in the community and a member of the DAR, being mortified when it was pointed out that she should not have used the flag to drape the buffet on which she was serving dinner!)
- Not the flag, but blue, white and red bunting should be used as decoration, with the blue on top, then white, and the red on the bottom.
- The flag should not be used for advertising purposes.
- It should not be displayed on cushions, handkerchiefs, napkins, or any other articles that will be discarded. (Oh, boy! How often have we— including yours truly—violated that rule!)
- The flag should not be used as part of a costume or athletic uniform. The exceptions are small flags sewn on the uniforms of the military, firemen, policemen and members of patriotic organizations.
- When the flag is lowered, it should not touch the ground or any other object: It is received by waiting hands and arms.

Happy Independence Day!

Manners
of mourning >

How one responds to someone
who has experienced the death of a
loved one may have changed customs
from past to present, but the words
shared still require care and
consideration.

Recently I attended several funerals, including two for very close relatives. In days gone by, the rules of mourning included severe restrictions on dress and behavior. Queen Victoria went into deep mourning, and wore black for the rest of her life after the death of her husband, Prince Albert.

Following Victoria's lead, her subjects devised complex rituals to memorialize their deceased. These mandated elaborate funerals and the withdrawal from social activities for a proscribed period of time. Excruciatingly strict rules concerning dress for men, women and children were also obligatory. As the mourning period progressed, colors became lighter, from black to grey to mauve. Fans of Downton Abbey will recall that Dowager Countess Violet always wore shades of grey, mauve, and beige, because she was widowed. These rules were universally known; people (bereaved or not) knew how to behave, dress and act.

Not so today. In our increasing casual society, most simply don't know what to wear to a funeral. What do we say to friends and co-workers who are grieving? Often we don't know – possibly because we don't want to face another's grief, and perhaps our own mortality.

What to do, say, and not say:

- At the funeral, dress appropriately to show respect for the deceased,
  the family, and yourself.
- Send a card or note to the family, and if you can, add a little something
  you remember about the deceased. This gesture will bring comfort to the family.
- Please don't co-mingle a condolence message with business.
- Don't say "if there is anything I can do, call me."
  A bereaved person will never call you.
- Saying "I am so sorry for your loss" sounds weak, but it is the best thing to say.
  Then be silent and listen.
- Never ask about details of the death. If the bereaved wants to share, they will.
- Although it sounds kind, don't ask "how are you doing?"
  Early on, most people haven't processed their grief enough to answer that question.
  They may not want to talk about their feelings to you. That question might elicit
  a wave of grief, and that's not your intention.
- Don't say "He or she is in a better place." That's not really our call, is it?
- Or "It was his or her time to go."—see above.
- Or "I know how you feel." Please don't say that, because you don't.

Understand that people deal with grief in different ways. Give them time and space to find their paths forward.

The inauguration of a president >

Radford University's inauguration of its new president reminds us of the importance of the occasion and how such events should be celebrated.

In October 2016, I had the privilege of attending the inauguration of Brian O. Hemphill, Ph.D. as the Seventh President of Radford University. The inauguration of a university president is a momentous occasion, not only for the institution and the new president, but for higher education throughout the world. President Hemphill's inauguration was full of pomp and circumstance as befitting the historic nature of the event. There were five distinct parts and symbols that were part of the ceremony.

The Academic Regalia: Part of the thrill of an inauguration is when the processional party enters in their vibrant academic robes.

The Processional: The party marched in to the stirring sounds of bagpipes, and consisted of the Chief Marshall (carrying the Mace), the color guard, students, learned societies, alumni, and faculty members, delegates from other colleges and universities, the university administration, members of the Board of Visitors, the platform party, and the Rector of the Board of Visitors escorting the President.

The Seal: University Seals harken back to the Middle Ages. The Seal is a legal mark, and one of the University's most significant symbols. The seal is incorporated into the inauguration both for its symbolism and legal significance.

The Mace: The Radford University Mace was presented to President Hemphill as a symbol of the authority vested in him by the Board of Visitors. The ceremonial mace was adopted in the late 16th century by academia, and is only used on formal occasions.

The Presidential Medallion: The Medallion, again, is a tradition dating from the middle ages. It was placed around the President's neck by the Rector of the Board of Visitors, symbolizing the authority vested in the office of the presidency by the Board.

It was an honor to attend a ceremony which continues one of the great traditions that reaches back through the centuries to medieval universities of Paris and Bologna. It was one full of pageantry, the protocol of which was planned out to the last detail. As professionals we will be invited to many formal events. We can appreciate an inauguration more if we understand its symbolism.

Let's segue to the upcoming Presidential Inauguration in January, 2017. You did not see the pageantry of an academic inauguration, but be sure protocol officers planned the event down to the minutest detail. The event characterized the civility with which governments change hands in our country. Despite the charged events that led up to the election, we saw the outgoing and incoming presidents being extremely civil to each other – that's the American way!

Hanging on to
the mantle of power >

Where do titles go after the person
no longer serves in that capacity?

Let's talk about honorifics. Honorifics? An elegant word we don't often use, but its meaning we use all the time. An honorific is a polite descriptive title we put before a person's name. Think President, Senator, Doctor, and Colonel — these are honorifics. When our children call their teachers Mr. Teachalot or Ms. Mathwhiz, they are using honorifics.

What about honorifics in government and political life, when the person no longer holds office? Robert Hickey, author of *Honor & Respect: The Official Guide to Names, Titles, and Forms of Address,* writes that the rules vary for former officials. He says that "for those who held offices filled by only one person at a time—such as president, vice president, secretary of state, and even governor or mayor—it is confusing to the public, and disrespectful to the current office holder, to hang onto the title." He adds "People with titles held concurrently by many, such as senators or judges, are not violating tradition by keeping their honorifics."

Emily Yoffe, columnist for *Slate*, put it more bluntly when she wrote "Politicians ... who cling to their old titles are pretentious, incorrect, and un-American." Goodness!

In April 1789, after a month-long debate, the senate proposed that our first president should be called "His Highness, the President of the United States of America, and Protector of their Liberties." This designation was refused on the grounds that it was unconstitutional. George Washington, after he returned to private life, chose his previous title "General." John Quincy Adams was President, Senator, Secretary of State, ambassador to many countries, and a member of the House of Representatives. Throughout his years of service, he was known simply and modestly as Mr. Adams. When Harry Truman was no longer president, he returned to Independence, Missouri, as Mr. Truman.

As with most protocol rules, though, there is an exception, and that is for members of the House. One hears Congressman Rattleson and Congresswoman Rambling, but those are not official titles. Members of the House of Representatives should be designated by their social title i.e. Mr. or Ms., Mrs., or Dr. That being said, the State Department's Office of Protocol seems resigned, admitting "The titles 'congressman' and 'congresswoman' are becoming more common in social usage, but are not, strictly speaking, correct forms of address." Mr. Hickey advises "... the best rule for any ex-official is, "Who are you at this moment?"

Nevertheless, keeping the appearance of power obviously has its advantages, and most find it difficult to surrender his or her honorific. It's a balance between what is correct, and what politicians like to be called. Now that you know the rules, you might have fun seeing who hangs on to their honorific and who does not!

How (not) to treat a guest speaker >

Both the speaker and the host need to be prepared for the engagement.

I was contracted to conduct a business etiquette seminar, which was to be followed by a four-course dining tutorial. I enjoy my work conducting these seminars, because I interact with exceptionally interesting professionals.

I had a single point of contact which, in order to maintain communications ahead of time, is very important for a visiting speaker. I carefully prepared my handouts, power point slides, and other materials for the seminar. I emailed everything to my contact person, with instructions for handling and asking for verification that everything was in order. I heard nothing back until I phoned and emailed several times. Hmmm—a portent of things to come?

I usually arrive early for my seminars. It's better to arrive with time to prepare calmly, and it is a courtesy to my client that they don't have to worry about when I'm going to show up. I did get caught up in unusually heavy traffic, but arrived well ahead of the appointed hour. Thank goodness I did. Very little had been prepared. The conference room was hot and had not been set up properly; the notebooks were not assembled, and the power point slides that I had sent via email were not there.

My host and I sprang into action: we found someone to adjust the temperature; we set up the room, and assembled the workbooks. Fortunately, I always carry a back-up flash drive, containing the current program's power point slides. A computer and projector were found and the slides installed. A number of participants were tardy, causing us to start late. This became problematic because we had a finite amount of time to complete the business etiquette part of the program, before the caterer was scheduled to serve dinner.

In the confusion, someone failed to introduce me, and so I plunged on. According to Communication Theorist, Dr. Nick Morgan "…a good introduction is essential to get a speaker off to a good start…it can help establish, credibility... trust and likability."

If you talk to enough professional speakers, you invariably will hear horror tales of things that went wrong before, during, and after their presentations. My story is certainly not a horror story. But was it stressful? You bet it was! Did I show it? I hope not. Remember: it's under trying circumstances that we rely on our automatic good manners to surface.

Moral of the story: the presenter has an obligation to be prepared, but so does the client!

Please respond! >

It's simple really—when
you're invited, you need to respond.

If you've ever hosted or planned a corporate event, a wedding, a business meal, even a party at your house, this article will resonate. If you haven't, as you grow in your profession, you will undoubtedly be asked to plan or host an event.

RSVP is French. "Répondez s'il vous plait" means, "Please reply." It is a request to inform your host as to whether or not (note the not) you intend to attend. Nowadays the courtesy of responding to an invitation is, sadly, in decline. People are responding less and less, and this phenomenon is widespread. I have seen hosts, event planners and administrative assistants, stressed and frustrated because guests have not responded. If an event is a large business luncheon, and less than 30% have responded, what is one to do when the caterer is asking for numbers? Be aware that caterers have deadlines to order food and assign staff to an event.

In times gone by people would respond to an invitation on personal stationery. They would "reply in kind" - in the style of the invitation. Today it is common to include response cards with an invitation, indicating a deadline for responding. Some are appalled by this – Miss Manners even calls response cards "horrid." Today phoning, texting, emailing, tweeting, LinkedIn and Facebook are all methods of responding.

RSVP Etiquette:

- Respond in the same form as the invitation—
  telephone, email, e-vite, or a good old-fashioned written note.
- Don't give lackadaisical replies such as
  "I'll come if nothing happens"—tacky!
- Never ask who else is coming—rude!
- "Regrets only" means the host assumes you will attend,
  unless you say otherwise.
- It is rude to ask to bring a guest.
  If your host intended that, it would be on the invitation.
- You could say, "I'm so sorry, my college roommate is visiting"
  and allow your host to say "So sorry you can't attend"
  or "Do bring her along."
- May a single person bring a guest to an event?
  Only if the invitation says "and guest."
- May the host phone and ask for a response?
  Yes, rules of etiquette change to fit the times.
  It is now appropriate to phone saying something like
  "...my caterer requests a firm number by tomorrow..."

Remember, responding to an invitation in a timely manner is an effective way for you to project yourself as a smart, savvy professional.

DEMOGRAPHIC SENSITIVITIES

Teach your children well >

Good manners begins with you teaching your children how to behave in a variety of circumstances.

When I started my business, clients came from the corporate world. They were mostly mid- to upper-level executives brought up in the 1970s and '80s when an "anything goes" mentality was in full force. As they climbed the corporate ladder, they found that they were hampered by a lack of social and dining skill.

Soon, many of these high powered people were asking me to train their children, admitting that they just didn't have the time or skills to do it themselves. I do not teach children's etiquette anymore, but here are my thoughts on the matter.

You will give your children an extra edge and the gift of a lifetime if you teach them manners and proper dining skills. Good manners leads to the kind of confidence that is needed for the development of a strong, confident child.

The well-mannered child:

- Practices kindness in dealing with others, the Golden Rule.
- Respects authority.
- Tries not to interrupt.
- Respects other religions and other cultures.
- Shakes hands easily.
- Makes good eye contact. (Many children are shy about making eye contact, so tell them about the "safe zone." i.e. the space between the eyebrows.)
- Knows the value of a "thank you" note. (Some colleges withhold disbursing scholarship money to students until the thank you letters from the recipients have been mailed to their donors.)
- Displays proper behavior in public places. (Don't subject those around you to screaming children—remove them.)
- Knows proper e-mail, telephone and cell phone etiquette.
- Demonstrates proper table manners: when to pick up a napkin, how to eat soup, how to hold a knife and fork properly.
- Knows that texting at the table is a no-no.

Encourage children to practice social and dining skills. Remind them that, if they play a musical instrument, they practice before a performance or a recital. The same is true with manners.

Teach your children the value of good manners, respect and proper dining etiquette. Those skills will last a lifetime.

Millennials
in the workplace >
(Part One)

How wide you see the
"generation gap" may well depend
on the extent of your information.

Many older, more traditional people in the professional arena are distrustful of these "Young Turks", who just don't seem to conform to the norm in the business world. Who are they anyway? Let's take a look at some of the characteristics of this generation, born between 1982 and 1998. They are having a huge impact on society, and they are changing the way the professional works. Some employers will need to adjust their policies and business practices to accommodate this new generation. This will include finding new ways to motivate and reward them.

Millennials say they would prefer to own a business, rather than be a top executive. They have a keen entrepreneurial sense that includes social entrepreneurship. A perfect example of a social entrepreneur is Blake Mycoskie, founder in 2006 of TOMS shoes. For every pair of shoes sold, TOMS donates a pair to someone in a developing country. In 2011, TOMS expanded its One for One concept to eyewear.

Sales of this newer product help the company donate eye glasses, and fund glaucoma surgeries for people in the developing world. To date, the company has donated more than 10 million pairs of shoes, and restored the eyesight of 200,000 people. By the way, there is no Tom. TOMS is derived from the word "tomorrow", and the hope that tomorrow will bring a better world.

As children many Millennials were catered to by family and school, and were told:

- "You are special." "You are smart."
- "You must achieve!" Some parents started choosing the right pre-school
  while the child was still in the womb. (If the reader thinks this begs credibility,
  be assured that this writer has witnessed the phenomenon!)
- "You must attend the 'right' college." Some parents hire private agents
  to find the "right" college.

In addition many Millennials:

- Are tolerant and inclusive—of races, religions, and sexual orientations.
- Are connected all the time with their computer, smart phone, and/or i-Pad.
- Prefer chatting on line to talking in person or on the phone.
- Believe in service to the community. Many high schools require
  community service hours for graduation.

In one national survey, where Millennials were asked for the major cause of problems in the country, they opined "selfishness." Yet some consider the millennial generation to be selfish, narcissistic, and lazy.

Obviously, not all Millennials are coddled. A huge number of the population lives in desperation and poverty. This will create its own set of problems in society. More of the Millennial story will be discussed in Part Two.

Millennials
in the workplace >
(Part Two)

Understanding attitudes
and perceptions goes a long way.

Millennials are a generation of workers with a completely different attitude towards work than any generation that has gone before. These sociable, optimistic, talented, well-educated, collaborative, open minded young people have characteristics that include:

- Self-confidence: raised by parents who nurtured self-esteem in their children, Millennials are supremely confident in their ability to overcome challenges. Employers and co-workers who respect years of experience, and "paying your dues" often find this attitude disturbing—even arrogant.
- Hopefulness: They believe in their ability to change the future. They like to be challenged, and to be well compensated for their work.
- Achievement oriented. An example is Olympic gold medal winner, Sarah Hughes, who announced the day following her victory that her next goal was to score 1600 on her College Board SATs.
- Inclusiveness: Millennials like working in teams. They have a finely honed sense of fairness, and they want no one left behind. They want their companies and corporations to have a social conscience and contribute to their communities.
- Civic-mindedness: They think of the greater good.

The rate of high school graduates who go to college and receive a degree is at an all-time high. This is good news for future employers.

However, there is a distinct concern about what has been called the digital divide—the gap between the "haves" and the "have not's." Never has the difference been so apparent, and this division is centered around technology. There is a large group of young people who are growing up without computers or access to computers—the great unifier of the Millennials. Companies like Microsoft have donated millions of dollars to make computers available to disadvantaged children. They are also spearheading mentoring and training programs for young people, but it is a daunting task.

How do employers proceed with programs that attract, retain, and motivate the Millennial employee? They should understand that:

- Millennials want leaders that display honesty and integrity.
- They want to be challenged.
- They want to work with friends. Some corporations are hiring groups of friends!
- They want respect for their ideas, even though they haven't spent years in the trenches.
- They want to work in a fun, collaborative environment.
- They want a flexible schedule. A rigid environment and work schedule is guaranteed to make your Millennial worker look elsewhere for employment.

The Millennials are a fascinating generation charged with potential! The savvy, resilient employer will welcome this creative energy into their midst!

Children
and restaurants >

Whether children should be at
fine dining establishments depends
on how they behave and what to do
when they don't; and the answer
could be as simple as: no.

"No strollers, no high chairs, no booster chairs. Children crying or making loud noises are a distraction to other diners, and as such are not allowed in the dining room" Thus said a sign in a fine restaurant in California. From LA to New York, higher end restaurants are setting age limits for children in their establishments, or even banning them outright! A little harsh? Perhaps, but nice for the grownups out for an enjoyable dining experience.

Here's my view on screaming babies and out of control children running around the restaurant or playing (ugh!) under tables. A nice restaurant is an adult environment. It has been my experience that parents do a disservice to young children by placing them in an adult situation where they are expected to behave as adults. As Miss Manners says"…you are being unfair, not only to other restaurant patrons, but to your own children…do not mislead yourself into thinking these outings are a treat for the children." I agree with her: it is misery for small children to be expected to sit, be quiet, talk softly, and use proper table manners. Most children under six or seven are simply not up to coping with that kind of stress.

Some parents of young children think that taking their children to nice restaurants helps them learn table manners. I suggest that the table manners should be learned at home, or in one of my classes! Dr. Richard Bromfield, a psychologist at Harvard Medical School and author of *How to Unspoil Your Child Fast: A Speedy Complete Guide to Contented Children and Happy Parents* has a different take from mine. He says "Yes, restaurants can be a learning experience for children, but no, other diners do not have to suffer through the lesson."

Here are some of his suggestions:

- Plan and share excitement about going out to dinner for several days beforehand.
- Clearly state the kind of behavior that is expected.
- If your child acts up or disrupts, calmly leave the restaurant without finishing dinner or taking food home.
- Leave without explanation, excuses or anger.
- On the way home, or later, do not yell at the child or punish for what happened. You will only undercut the power of your strong parenting deed.

Confident, courteous, respectful children are what we're after here. It does take strong parenting to do any or all of the actions suggested above. But then, who said parenting was a walk in the park?

Children
and the holidays >

Perhaps it's time to reevaluate
your holiday traditions.

Looking at the TV ads and the dazzling magazine spreads depicting perfect holidays, brimming with happily smiling children, I reflected on the reality that some families experience during the season. We've all seen or lived it –bored, scowling children, children having temper tantrums, unhappy with their presents, unhappy with their parents, unhappy with themselves.

Why do we feel the need to indulge our children at Christmas, Hanukkah, Kwanzaa, or any other special holiday? Some psychologists suggest that we relive our own childhood, and either want it to replicate our experience if it was happy, or make it better if it was unhappy. Maybe so, but I think television and social media have a lot to do with the pressure on parents to provide more and more of everything – including holiday gifts.
Remember dreaming of that bicycle or doll, or special book, and hoping and praying that it would appear until the tree? Children really don't seem to do that anymore. Perhaps that's because they know that parents and grandparents will provide them with just about anything they want. Maybe we are not doing our children a service by overindulging them. I confess I'm as guilty of that as anyone!

It might be time to reset and:

- Teach the children the value of generosity at holiday time.
    Generosity of not just gifts, but of time.
- Help them to choose gifts for a toy drive, or sponsor a less fortunate family.
- Volunteer as a family at a shelter that serves meals at holiday time.
- Invite someone new or who is all alone to a holiday meal.
- Help your children make cookies or little gifts
- Visit a nursing home with these gifts. Holidays are a very hard time
    for these patients, and they would love to see a child's face.
- This is not easy to do, I know. Princess Diana took her boys
    to homeless shelters to teach them compassion at a very young age.
- Make memories for your children at holiday time by decorating together.
- Welcome the carolers!
- Take the family to a holiday program at your local high school.
- Encourage the children to remember those who are not home
    for the holidays—especially our troops.
- Make your traditions unique to your family.

Remember, children simply love ritual and tradition. They will recall the traditions and memories long after the popular toy of the season has been forgotten.

Disability or handicap? >

Engagement and interaction between an individual with a disability and one who does not have that same challenge can require some considerations.

I've often thought about writing about people with disabilities: how we react to them and treat them, and what is considered to be the correct term. We all probably know someone who has a physical, mental, sight or hearing disability. My cousin is wheelchair bound due to an accident, and I have a brilliant colleague who is blind. I have spoken at length to both, as well as others, while preparing this book.

What is the correct or appropriate terminology? Is it disability or handicap? Starting in the early 20th century, handicapped was the preferred term for physical and mental issues. The American with Disabilities Act was passed in 1990, and the word "handicapped" began to seem discourteous.

Many people feel awkward around those with disabilities because we are nervous about saying or doing the wrong thing. It's important to remember that, as in any population, people with handicaps are all different. Some prefer different labels, some get annoyed about labels, and some could simply not care less.

Disabled workers are being welcomed into the workplace in increasing numbers. A current television series The Good Doctor features a brilliant young surgeon who has autism. In the real world Microsoft actively seeks workers along the autism spectrum because "It's a talent pool that really hasn't been tapped," said Jenny Lay-Flurrie, the chief accessibility officer at the tech giant located outside of Seattle. Ms. Lay-Flurrie, who is profoundly deaf, added "People with disabilities are a strength and a force of nature in this company, myself included."

Some things to keep in mind:

- Be aware of personal space. If a person uses a wheelchair or walker,
  it is part of their personal space. Ask before you touch or move these aids.
- Ask before you help. Most persons with a disability will be very specific as to
  whether they do or do not want help. They will tell you what they want or need.
- Talk directly to the person instead of a caregiver or interpreter.
- If a person is in a wheelchair: ask if he or she would like you to sit
  rather than stand to talk.
- Please don't play with service dogs! These wonderful animals are highly trained
  to assist their owner with important tasks. Always ask permission before you
  approach a service dog. Don't be surprised if the owner says "no." My friend
  who is blind often says "Not now if you don't mind, my dog is working
  at the moment, and can't be disturbed."

In most cases, the operative word is "ask."

LOOKING GOOD

A tip of the hat >

Wearing hats, including baseball caps,
requires attention to the rules.

Have you noticed that more men are wearing hats these days? When I teach business etiquette classes in colleges and universities, I am always struck by the number of young men who attend class wearing baseball caps. Most are baffled when I ask them to remove their headgear. They find it curious when I explain that removing one's hat indoors is a traditional sign of respect.

If you look at old movies from the thirties, forties, and fifties, you'll notice that all men wore hats. Some say President John F. Kennedy triggered the decline in the wearing of hats, and thus the decline of a whole industry, when he appeared hatless at his inauguration on a bitter cold January day in 1961. That, technically, is not true; there are photographs of President Kennedy, wearing a high silk hat to and from his inauguration. The elegant topper was clearly visible on his chair as he delivered his inaugural address. There is little doubt, though, that President Kennedy usually preferred to go hatless.

The custom of removing one's hat seems to date back to mediaeval times when knights either lifted their visors or removed their helmets entirely in order to identify themselves. Failure to do so could have fatal consequences.

It is true that hats are no longer a necessary part of a wardrobe, but they are coming back into fashion for both men and woman. There are some pretty specific etiquette rules for men wearing hats, but not so many for women. So let's look at the rules, which I admit, like most things, are changing:

A man can leave his hat on:
- Outdoors
- At athletic events
- On public transport
- On elevators
- In public buildings e.g., the post office, hotel lobbies

He should, however, remove his hat, and this includes baseball caps:
- In a private home
- At mealtimes
- When being introduced – that's both indoors and outdoors
- In a Christian place of worship
- While at work indoors
- In schools, libraries, courthouses, town halls
- In restaurants
- At movies or indoor performances (women also, if the hat is big!)
- When the National Anthem is being played
- When the U.S. Flag passes by, e.g. in a parade

Remember, removing a hat at the appropriate time, like standing for a superior, is a mark of respect and courtesy.

Tattoos >

To tat or not to tat may not be
the question; it might just be how,
when or where.

Lest we think tattooing is a modern practice, let's take a quick peak into history. Mankind has always enjoyed adorning the body with art, and the practice dates back to at least 6000 BC to South America. History also tells us that the first documented tattoo artist in America tattooed soldiers on both sides during the Civil War

Let's fast forward and discuss tattoos in the workplace. Not too long ago a parent would admonish, "You'll never get a job with that tattoo!" Today, tattoos have undoubtedly become more accepted in mainstream America. Businesswise, as companies stress their commitment to inclusion and diversity, tattoos are becoming less taboo in some workplaces. If you want to hire a lot of Millennials, better get comfortable with tattoos!

I spoke to several professionals responsible for hiring and firing. One said, "...Just because you think it's your right to have tattoos doesn't mean it's smart to display them." Another, the head of a law office with over 100 lawyers, dismissed the idea out of hand. "If I see a tattoo, I don't hire.' Another, an office manager in a large firm, said "I don't care if I can't see them."

Smart professionals should consider their goals when it comes to a job search or advancing a career. They need to think about whether their "tats" will risk their chance of landing a position or of moving up the career ladder.

So what is more important? Is it one's freedom of expression or a career? By the way, some think that tattoos are protected by the First Amendment, but beware; the federal government does not protect tattoos under the First Amendment.

Some suggestions:

- Be aware of the cultural values in the workplaces
  in which you see yourself working.
- Be aware that there are certain "conservative" cultures
  that may not tolerate visible tattoos, no matter how small.
  These include the legal, accounting, engineering and medical professions.
- Be aware of regional differences in attitudes. Southwest Virginia is not LA!
- Be aware that age has something to do with attitudes towards tattoos:
  the older the employer, the more likely he or she will dislike them.

Remember there are countless ways to express yourself as a distinctive person. If tattooing is your choice, go for it, but consider placing them where you can cover them up. You don't want to create a permanent barrier to your career, do you?

What to wear >

First impressions matter;
they simply do.

"What am I going to wear?" is an age old lament. And, down through the centuries, dress codes—often numbingly strict—have ruled and railed and insisted on telling us how to package ourselves.

We've all heard that first impressions are lasting. Allison Lurie in her book *The Language of Clothes* writes in an almost lyrical manner "Long before I am near enough to talk to you…you announce your sex, age, and class to me through what you are wearing—and very possibly give me important information (or misinformation!) as to your occupation, origin, personality, opinions, tastes…by the time we meet and converse, we have already spoken to each other in an older and more universal tongue."

Sometimes the younger generation has a difficult time accepting the fact that they are judged by that first impression—by what they wear and how they present themselves. They want to be judged by their stellar inner traits, education, and accomplishments. Unfortunately, stellar inner traits, education and accomplishments are not visible immediately, and take time to reveal themselves. That's when we're left with the first impression —and that takes about 5 to 7 seconds.

I advise my clients to dress to the culture in which they are working. For instance, if they are going into a conservative culture such as banking, accounting or the legal profession, it's best to dress conservatively. Doing that demonstrates an understanding of the profession and its particular corporate culture. After all, we really wouldn't have much faith in our lawyer or banker, or even our doctor, if they showed up dressed for the gym. On the other hand, if one is in a creative profession such as theatre, art, graphic design or rock music, it wouldn't do to show up dressed like a banker. The person's creative flair would definitely be questioned.

Think of the theatre or the movies: when an actor or actress appears on stage or on screen, we know almost immediately what kind of character they are before they say the first word. The actors have been packaged or costumed so that the audience knows what they are and who they are. A very simple example: the innocent heroine is never dressed in a short, tight, red dress, but the vixen almost invariably is!

It's a similar thing in the various professions. In our work lives we show our professionalism—or lack thereof —by our appearance. Understanding that is one of the first hurdles we face as we enter the workforce.

Now all that being said…today's rules are rapidly changing. We'll address that later!

Neckties
and bowties >

There's a reason these accessories
have survived for so long; better pay
attention.

"Show me a man's ties, and I'll tell you who he is or who he is trying to be," writes John T. Molloy in his book *Dress for Success*. Molloy conducted experiments showing that men wearing expensive ties make stronger impressions in job interviews, are given better tables at restaurants and even make more money panhandling. Although this writer must say that she has never seen a panhandler wearing a tie – expensive or otherwise!

Nevertheless, the necktie as we know it has been a staple in men's wear since the early twentieth century. Little boys protest wearing them; most men can't wait to untie them after a long day's work, and most women like to see their men wearing them.

What is it about the necktie that survives the decades? Although real sartorial gurus will differ with me here, I don't think men's suits, jackets, blazers, or trousers change that much when it comes to showing an individual's style. But the tie – now there is the accessory that reveals personality, individuality, character, sense of humor, or even one's place in the world. Think of the "old school tie" the "club tie" or the "regimental" tie.

In the past few decades turtlenecks, shirts without ties, and the influence of casual startup companies threatened to derail neckwear. However, despite these threats, in the worldwide business arena, neckties are still required. So, make sure your ties are of good quality silk. Learn which knot suits your shirt and neck best. Don your tie – and conquer your world!

Now let's consider the bowtie! This nifty little piece of neckwear, its origins dating back to the 17th century, has made a huge comeback in the past few years. It is usually worn by men who are not afraid to step up their game when it comes to fashion. The bowtie implies a savvy sophistication – think of James Bond. It can transform an otherwise dull ensemble into one that exudes poise and self-confidence.

Bowties are prevalent in the workplace these days; however I wouldn't recommend wearing one for the first interview for a job. Wait until you get the position before unleashing your bevy of bowties in the workplace!

There are many ways to wear a bowtie, but you just need to know the best way. No pre-tied or clip on bowties for you! Learn to tie your bowtie yourself. It will never look perfect like the pre-tied sort, but that's the look you want.

"A well-tied tie is the first serious step in life."—Oscar Wilde

Casual Fridays >

Be careful not to take the
"dress down day" too far.

I think we can all agree that business dress, like technology, is changing and evolving at lightning speed. Up until the last fifteen years or so, all businesses required their professional workers to dress in a formal way. Suits, shirts, ties for men; dresses and skirted suits for woman. In fact, it wasn't until the last decade that pant suits became completely acceptable for professional women to wear in the workplace.

A few decades ago, "Casual Fridays" or "Dress Down days" started on the West Coast as a way of encouraging creativity and improving morale. No surprise there, as the West Coast is considered to have a more casual culture.

Like many good ideas, this one had unintended consequences. Some older, more seasoned, workers became uncomfortable without their formal attire, while younger workers enthusiastically embraced the idea. According to noted author, Dr. Jeffrey L. Magee, an added issue was that, "relaxed dress codes lead to relaxed manners...relaxed productivity." Maybe so. I have a relative who telecommutes from Los Angeles to Washington every day. She could work in her pajamas since no one really sees her. Nevertheless, she dresses as if going to a regular office. She says she feels more put together and more productive.

Employers became alarmed when dress down Fridays became an excuse for sloppy and inappropriate attire. Then recently, to add to the confusion, "Dress Up Thursdays" appeared on the horizon to counter "Casual Fridays." No doubts about it, a lot of professionals are baffled when deciding what to wear these days.

I was contracted by a nationally known, rather conservative, corporation to talk specifically about appropriate dress in the workplace. Good and reliable employees, usually the younger ones, were showing up in totally inappropriate attire. The women were guilty of the most mistakes - probably because they have more choices – but the men weren't off the hook either!

So for the professional women: relegate the heavy makeup; the too short skirts; the revealing necklines; the cropped tops; the large dangling jewelry, and the strappy stiletto heels, to your personal life. Dressing professionally will increase your credibility in your workplace.

As for the men: wear the worn jeans; the jogging outfit; the cowboy boots; the running shoes; the baseball caps, and generally sloppy clothing, when you're relaxing on your own time. You will gain added respect if you dress appropriately.

"Look around the workplace, see how successful people dress, and imitate. I'll bet you won't find senior level folks dressed shabbily – or in flip-flops."—Elizabeth Freedman

Professional dressing >

Professional attire equates with
"credibility" in the business world.

There's a lot of confusion these days about what is and is not professional dressing. Fashions go in and out of style at a dizzying pace, and many are seduced into purchasing garments that are just plain inappropriate. In a traditional or conservative profession the rules haven't really changed much, so it's much easier to dress appropriately. The problem is that many young people, fresh out of college, just don't want to conform to what they perceive is an old-school workplace.

Make no mistake: if you work client-oriented professions — the legal, accounting, finance, insurance, sales, (and dare I say it?) funeral professions — in order to be perceived as credible, you must dress the part. The rules are very simple and easy to follow for both men and women.

Women: Skirted suits, or tailored pantsuits, and good quality blouses. Good leather closed toe pumps complete the ensemble. Avoid too much make-up, too much hair, and too much jewelry. Note: in the past few years it has become routine not to wear hose with skirts and dresses. Hmmm…here it's best check out what's going on in your office.

For Men: Mid to dark colored suits, white, blue or cream colored shirts with a silk tie that has a pop of color. Good quality leather shoes and belt complete the ensemble. Note: shoes and belt should be the same color, and the tie should land near the middle of the belt. Avoid wearing jewelry, except a watch. Tie bars have become popular again with classic clothes. I'm not an enthusiast, but if you do wear one, make sure you learn the proper size to choose and how to wear it properly.

Now that we've gotten that out of the way, let's consider the "why" of dressing professionally. In addition to remembering what Albert Mehrabian's research on communication revealed: namely that "55% of a message is transmitted by the speaker's appearance and body language," other factors come in to play:

- Looking the part enhances self-confidence and self-esteem.
- Looking the part affords you credibility with clients and management.
- Rightly or wrongly, well dressed people are often perceived as leaders.
- Dress for the job you want, not the job you're in. In other words, if you are a manager, looking to be an executive, then dress like an executive.

Remember, it's still all about first impressions. We are judged by how we act and how we look. Dressing appropriately gives one a competitive advantage.

"The rulers of corporate America wear suits—always have, always will."—John Malloy, author of *Dress for Success*

LET'S TALK

The art of
the written note >

The hand-written note:
"A gesture of kindness and civility."

In Victorian times, when there was no e-mailing, texting, tweeting or Facebook postings, the art of letter writing became a fine art, indeed. Victorians wrote charming, heartfelt letters and effusive notes for all occasions. The level of sentiment (and sentimentality) could be extraordinary. These scripts, written with perfect handwriting or calligraphy, were often accompanied by elaborate drawings and flourishes.

We don't go to those extravagant lengths anymore, but I must admit I am pleased when I see a hand addressed envelope appear in my mail box!. When someone has sat down with pen in hand to write a letter to me, it makes me feel a whole lot more valued than when I receive a message on my computer.

In this frenetic world, some think that a quick telephone call or e-mail of thanks is enough. It is not. A written expression of appreciation is a courtesy, whether written to a friend, a family member or a business associate. I recently received a "thank you" note from my grandson, thanking me and his grandfather for his birthday presents. It occurred to me it was no accident that this boy wrote this little note. Before he was old enough to write, his mother always wrote lovely notes to thank us for his gifts, and he would sign them with a little squiggle.

The written note is a gesture of kindness and civility, and it can be as short as three sentences. The first sentence typically expresses thanks for the occasion or gift. The second acknowledges the event or gift, and the third might talk about a future meeting. It only takes a few minutes.

The written note can be a valuable tool for the professional. It demonstrates social skills in a warm, personal fashion. It can help cement a business relationship, reverse a negative situation or create a positive new one.

Try writing a note to:

- Invite a potential client to meet with you
- Thank someone for a gift or favor
- Offer condolences to a friend or associate
- Thank someone after lunch, dinner or a meeting
- Congratulate a colleague on an honor, promotion, or award
- Acknowledge a milestone of a colleague
- Thank the interviewer after a job interview or
- Offer an apology (learn to grovel)

Ralph Waldo Emerson wrote. "Life is short, but there is always time for courtesy." Writing letters has become a lost art, but we can still show courtesy and civility by getting into the habit of penning a nice note on quality note cards.

Cell phone
and texting manners >

Let's face it. It's not the device
that's the problem. It's how we use it.

In January, 2012 at the Lincoln Center, during a performance of Mahler's Ninth Symphony, a cell phone rang for nearly five minutes. Conductor, Alan Gilbert, finally put down his baton and stopped the performance. The sophisticated (sic.) audience hurled abuse at the culprit (not good form either, wouldn't you agree?) and a national debate ensued on cell phones in performances.

We've all seen it—the child texting during dinner; the young business person talking on the cell phone during meetings, and yes, even us baby boomers sliding into senior citizen status sometimes do it. It seems that each generation has its own reasons for violating the rules for cell phoning and texting. It's almost a "You shouldn't do it, but I can—just this once." scenario. Let's face it. It's not the device that's the problem. It's how we use it.

Cell phones and texting are wonderful tools. I love my mobile device, which gives me freedom to work anywhere in the world I happen to be. I actually wrote and sent my first column for the FRONT on my mobile device while I was on a cruise.

When a child or adult texts or phones in the company of others, they are not giving attention to the people they are with. It's up to the parents to teach good mobile device manners. That said, it means we have to model that behavior to the children, and follow our own rules.

Cell phone and texting tips:

- Be present.
  Whether it's a conversation, a meeting, a dinner or a performance,
  put your phone on silent, and live in the moment.
- Be private.
  Don't tell the world about your private life. People don't really care,
  and it's rude to interrupt and intrude on others with loud talk.
- Be cool.
  Angry outbursts in public reflect poorly on us and embarrass others.
- Be quiet.
  Please doesn't "cell yell." Let's modulate our voices.
- Be polite.
  Stay at least 10 feet away from another person when talking.
- Be aware of latency.
  This electronic delay between when you speak and when the other person
  hears you is becoming more problematic as cell phone use increases.
  It can lead to one person repeatedly interrupting another. Apologize if you
  detect latency. That tells your caller that you don't mean to interrupt,
  and you are not being rude.
- Be focused.
  (Do I need to mention this?) Please don't text and drive.

Mea culpa! >

If you're writing a letter of apology,
it's best to mean it.

The phenomena of public apologies gained much of its traction in 1952, with the first nationally publicized television mea culpa by the late President Nixon, then the vice presidential running mate of President Eisenhower. Nixon, with his wife Pat watching pensively, denied charges that he gave special treatment to his donors. He did, however, apologize for accepting a little cocker spaniel dog named Checkers, saying, "We're gonna keep it."

This speech was seen by about 60 million Americans, resulting in a landslide of support. Nixon retained his spot as the vice presidential candidate, and his ticket won the election. The public apology is commonplace now. Politicians, sports figures and entertainers, usually with their spouses (but not always, these days) standing stoically beside them, offer public apologies for their errant behavior. To save a career or an election, they've had armies of public relations experts coaching them on dress, body language, and how to deliver a timely, sincere public apology.

Please note the word "sincere" here. As any person in sales can tell you, clients spot insincerity very quickly. While we're at it, let's remind ourselves that children can spot insincerity even faster.

Most of us will never have to apologize publicly. Being merely human, we all make mistakes and blunders that could cost us our reputation and/or our company's money. I was asked recently to help a client write a note of apology. This person really didn't want to write the note nor accept responsibility for the error. Well, that feeling certainly shone through. The note was full of "I'm sorry if I offended you ..." and "I apologize if I caused any trouble with your customer ..." And then there were excuses.

This approach will never do if one wants to repair a relationship. My unhappy client was forgetting good customer service, and the old adage that the client is always right. In a situation like this, promptly accepting responsibility is the best course. If you have made a mistake causing damaged relationships, consternation, and/or loss of profit, it's best to:

• Handwrite an apology immediately.
• Keep your letter short.
• Keep your tone honest and respectful.
• Sincerely acknowledge whatever harm your action caused.
• Sincerely apologize – no ifs, buts or excuses here.
• Sincerely offer to remedy the situation.

The apology letter is hard to write, and no one likes admitting to being less than perfect. Write it anyway. You'll feel better and so will the person receiving it.

The art
of conversation >

Small talk not your strong suit?
Your future may depend on it, so
practice, practice, practice.

I conducted a dining etiquette seminar for graduating college students to prepare them for the impending interview lunch or dinner. During such a seminar, I encourage questions throughout the meal, assuring them that there are no "dumb" or "silly'" questions.

When I said that ease of conversation or the ability to make small talk is essential during an interview meal – indeed in all business interactions - several students said that they were uncomfortable with this, and asked for help. Let's face it, making good conversation can be hard work, especially if some people don't understand that everyone has to contribute to, and participate in, the process.

There are some who worry that we are losing our ability to have lively, meaningful conversation. This may be connected with the widespread use of texting, tweeting and other social media to communicate. Some tips to hone our conversational skills:

- Understand that becoming a good conversationalist means doing your part in the conversation.
- Ask questions, but not personal ones. Asking questions shows your interest in the other person, their opinions or experiences.
- Ask follow-up questions to keep the conversation going.
- Hint: most people, even if they are shy, will talk about their hobbies, their children and their pets.
- Avoid questions that will elicit a yes/no answer, which stops conversation.
- Avoid topics that have the potential to polarize—and yes, I do mean politics and religion!
- Avoid talking about your health, how you slept, your diet—it's boring.
- Avoid talking about money. That's considered vulgar in some circles.
- Listen actively.
- Use body language, facial expressions, eye contact, and back-channeling to tell the other person that you are interested (or not) in what they are saying.
- Back-channeling is what we do through nodding, smiling and listening noises such as mmm-hmm. This lets others see that we are engaged and interested.
- Avoid monopolizing a conversation. That turns a dialogue into a monologue.
- Generate a list of topics to use with people who can't or won't converse. Sports, travel, music—there are a myriad of topics.
- With international guests, ask intelligent questions about their country, or make observations that show your knowledge of their culture. It's flattering to the visitor and there's never a lag in the conversation.

Remember there's a wonderful, fascinating world out there. And the key to unlocking the mysteries of it might just take the form of the person with whom you are conversing!

Body talk >

Body language is probably the most
revealing form of communication—
and it's always happening.

"When the eyes say one thing, and the tongue another, a practiced man relies on the language of the first."—Ralph Waldo Emerson

Historians tell us that the spoken word appeared 160,000 – 350,000 years ago. Prior to that, in more ancient times, communication was with gestures and grunts. All cultures instinctively share and understand body language. For example, if we landed in a foreign land where no one spoke our language, we could successfully get help with food, clothing, shelter, and directions without using a single word.

Research shows that facial emotions are the same in every culture: surprise, fear, anger, sadness, disgust, and happiness. Psychologist Paul Ekman, added a seventh – contempt. Some think they can evaluate people by watching their faces, but that is not the most reliable indicator of true feelings. The entire body tends to be more truthful than our faces. I can hide my feelings with a smile, but if my feet are turned to the door, my body language is saying, "I want out!" That is called "leakage." True feelings are leaking out. Experts can detect even small leaks! They can tune into body language and detect "micro-expressions" – brief changes in the face or gestures that show our true inner feeling. These happen so quickly that the layman might not notice. Successful salespeople have this ability, often without training.

"I speak two languages, Body and English."—May West, Actress

Truths about Body Language:
Body Language is a constant: you are always communicating. Appropriate body Language is determined by context—the social rules—the situation. What's acceptable in one social situation might not be acceptable in another. For example: it's fine to wink at your daughter at her recital, but not at the Queen of England, as one former President did!

Body language and speech should be congruent. In other words our words and our body language should not be at odds or incongruent. If you say "Hello, I'm really glad to meet you." with a limp handshake while looking past the person, you are really saying the opposite. According to psychologist Albert Mehrabian, words account for 7% of the message, tone of voice accounts for 38%, and body language account for 55%. Helpful Hint: If you want to signal that you are trustworthy, here is some body language that you could cultivate:

- Palms-up gestures
- Direct eye-contact
- Uncrossed arms
- Feet flat on the floor
- Erect posture
- Smiling
- Mirroring another's gestures.

Observe your colleague's body language at your next meeting. You will learn a lot!

What's up
with up speak? >

It's not just what you say but how you
say it that can impact one's perception
of your competence and credibility.

Let's talk about up speak. Up speak occurs when the speaker raises the voice at the end of a sentence. The trait has become more widespread among young woman, although men do it too. Women who speak this way could be viewed as less serious, less authoritative, and perhaps less intelligent. Not very fair, is it? But could this way of speaking hinder a young person's career?

In my business protocol seminars, designed to help participants present themselves with confidence and authority, I stress the importance of proper speech, tone, and grammar. Author John Baldoni, an internationally recognized leadership consultant wrote "For a young woman climbing the career ladder, how you sound will influence—rightly or wrongly— how you are perceived. (And the same applies to men.)"

Baldoni: "The sound of one's voice is linked to one's presence. We expect our leaders to demonstrate it [presence]. The sound of one's voice is what creates the first impression. The male voice ... is the de facto standard to which both women and men are compared. Judged by this standard, up speak is a killer."

Journalist Jessica Grose, when interviewing an older man for Businessweek, was told that "she sounded like his granddaughter." This was not meant as a compliment! "That was the first moment I felt [my voice] was hurting my career beyond just irritating a couple listeners," Grose told Fresh Air's Terry Gross. She did seek help from a speech coach, but stopped because "I felt like it was blunting my emotional range."

Back to Baldoni: "If you think or have been told that your voice is distracting due to up speak, work with a voice coach ... you are not changing you. You are modifying your vocalization so your inner self is projected credibly."

Dr. Penny Eckert, of Stanford University, thinks upspeak may have a generational aspect. She said, "I was shocked the first time I heard this style on NPR. I thought, 'How can this person be talking like this on the radio?' Then I played it for my students. I said, 'How does she sound?' They said, 'Good, authoritative.' And that was when I knew that I had a problem ... that I was not a part of the generation that understood what that style means. There's been a change and those of us who are bothered by some of these features are probably just getting old."

Which begs the question: Will young up speaking professionals hinder their prospects with potential employers who are usually "older?" Well, sounding like a grandchild certainly won't project confidence and authority!

Emailing
the professor >

There are proper ways to email
your professor; and it includes advice
you can carry with you into the
business world.

I think colleges and universities, and of course, students, jumped on the electronic bandwagon earlier than other populations. Online courses, online examinations, online questions to and from professors are the norm now. As Commencement approaches, and the pressure mounts, here are some observations and advice for students emailing their professors. And in the case of businesspeople, you also can use these tips when emailing other professionals.

- Save the texting, instant messaging, and Facebook posts for friends, family and fellow students.
- Caution: once sent, emails are out there forever.
- Send your email from your college or university account. wildchild@hotspa.com will undoubtedly get deleted before opening.
- Professors receive scores of emails a day. To ensure proper consideration of yours, put useful language in the subject line, e.g. class number, time, and a brief reason for your email.
- Check the syllabus before asking questions about things like office hours.
- Never make demands in your subject line e.g. "immediate response required," or "get back to me as soon as possible." Like you and me, professors react poorly to demands.
- Use a proper salutation e.g. Dear Dr. Finance or Dear Professor Economics. Formality is best, unless told otherwise. Starting off with "hi" or "hey" implies an intimacy that is not appropriate.
- Be clear and concise with your request. Number your questions, and if they are too convoluted, consider a meeting during office hours.
- Organize your emails with proper paragraph breaks, and your emails should be grammatically correct with no spelling mistakes.
- No ranting or whining! Rants and whines are not fun to read, and will probably elicit a negative response. Do not write in CAPITALS. That is considered shouting. .
- Unless otherwise instructed, don't send attachments.
- Resist the urge to make comments about his or her presentation style in class. Do that during evaluations at the end of the semester.
- Signatures matter. End by thanking your professor and use a respectful closing.
- Be sure to acknowledge and thank your professor when he/she gives you the information you requested. Doing so not only shows respect and courtesy, but also acknowledges that you have received the information.

Now, all that being said, nothing changes when you go graduate and go out into the demanding world of business and industry. Treat your bosses like I advise you to treat your professors – with civility, organization and discipline.

Personal questions >

Attend enough social gatherings,
and sooner than later you're apt to be
confronted with a personal question;
there are ways to diffuse such
intrusions.

When I conduct dining skills seminars for professionals, along with instructions on holding silverware, what to do with the napkin, or how to properly butter a roll, I include advice on conversation at the table. You know: avoid sensitive topics like religion and politics (oh, boy!), and I usually mention that it's best to avoid personal questions. I am often met with a blank stare and asked, "What's a personal question?"

Social media guarantees that almost nothing is sacred. Just about every detail of our personal lives—births, marriages, deaths, and everything in between—are advertised universally. It seems that no detail is too small or intimate to be broadcast far and wide.

What then is a personal question? Well, what about: "How come you're not married?" "When are you going to have a baby?" "How much did you pay for your house [or your car, or your clothes}?" "How much money do you earn?" Or "How did he/she die?" And what about "Why are you taking the day off from work?" "You've gained a lot of weight, haven't you?" "You look tired. Are you sick?" "Why are you getting a divorce?"

I'll allow that some people don't mind answering intrusive questions. However, there are many of us who become very uncomfortable when friends, co-workers or even "kind" relatives probe us with insensitive or just plain rude questions.

How do we respond to inappropriate questions? Probably our first reaction is to feel affronted, if only internally. Here we might want to remember that it is easy to exhibit good manners when everything is going well. It's harder when the situation is awkward or we're offended or even angry. That's when our automatic (practiced!) manners should kick in. Then our own kind but firm boundaries calmly can be set.

To all of the above questions, one could reply - with a smile—"I'm sorry, that's personal." or "Did you really mean to ask me that?" Remember a kind tone is important here. How you say it is just as important as what you say. My favorite response, though, is to pause for several beats, smile, and say "Excuse me, what did you ask?" When the question is repeated, I laugh happily, and say "That's what I thought you asked!" and pleasantly change the subject!

The renowned etiquette expert, Emily Post, wrote "Manners are a sensitive awareness of the feelings of others. If you have that awareness, you have good manners, no matter what fork you use."

The power of words >

Watch what you say and how
you say it; the words you use, matter.

Have you ever considered that the words we use when speaking to family, friends and coworkers can have long lasting positive or negative effects? Why is it that, for most of us, negative words from a boss or a colleague can affect us so much that months of praise are diminished or even forgotten?

According to Judith E. Glaser, Chair of The Creating WE Institute, and Richard D. Glaser, PhD in Biochemistry and founding member of the Institute, "Chemistry plays a big role in this phenomenon [forgetting the history of praise after experiencing one negative exchange]. When we face criticism, rejection or fear, when we feel marginalized or minimized, our bodies produce higher levels of cortisol, a hormone that shuts down the thinking center of our brains and activates conflict aversion and protection behaviors."

Mohammed Qahtani, Toastmasters 2015 World Champion of Public Speaking, said "A simple choice of word can make the difference between someone accepting or denying your message. You can have a very beautiful thing to say, but say it in the wrong words and it's gone. Words have power. Words are power."

We are bombarded with the concept of political correctness which, according to one definition, is "the idea that people should be careful to not use language… that could offend a particular group of people." Well, enough about that!
As we text or tweet, we are limited to the number of words we can use. According to Dr. Frank Luntz , in his New York Times best seller *Words that Work: It's Not What You Say, it's What People Hear*, the brevity of these communications "have a tendency to make in-hibitions go away… resulting in misunderstandings, hurt feelings."

In addition to our words, tone is important – how we say it is just as important as the words we use. A simple "thank you" can be insulting if said in an ugly or sarcastic tone.

Just as with some rules of etiquette, primary meanings of words change over time. Let's consider just two. The word "intercourse" was commonly considered "communication or dealings between individuals or groups" as in "everyday social intercourse." The word "gay" was commonly thought of as "lighthearted and carefree" as in, "We were merry and gay at the picnic." Both definitions are still correct, but most of us would shy away from using those meanings in everyday conversation.

So, are we choosing the right words and giving enough thought to what we send out? The words we use, whether oral or written, have tremendous power. They can build up or shatter relationships, both personally and professionally. Something to ponder in these an-tagonistic times, don't you think?

Listen up! >

Listening is so important,
we may need to practice or employ
some techniques to improve our skills.

I heard an interview with Celeste Headlee, author of *We Need to Talk: How to Have Meaningful Conversations*. Ms. Headlee, citing research, maintained that humans are not biologically designed to listen and retain information well. In fact, we retain only 50% of what we hear, and that percentage goes down quickly with each passing day. Ms. Headlee further opines that humans have an attention span of eight seconds, which is one second less that a goldfish! How this is calculated beats me, but there you have it.

We speak at about 200 words a minute, yet we can listen up to 500 words a minute. So unless we maintain focus, and that takes continuing energy, our active brains are wondering, thinking random thoughts, or about what we're going to say next—in other words we're not listening.

Listening has been called the missing half of communication, and one of the least used and undervalued skills of leaders and managers. Stephen Covey, author of *The 7 Habits of Highly Effective People* said "Most of us don't listen with the intent to understand, but with the intent to reply."

Social media, emailing, texting, multi-tasking—all take our attention away from conversational and listening skills. The Pew Research Center found that one third of U.S. teens text 100 times a day. Many people now prefer to text rather than talk. And before we shake our heads and "tut tut," let us adults admit that we are guilty too!

Listening actively is an acquired skill, even an art, and it takes constant practice. Let's start with an introduction. Many of us complain that we can't remember names. That may be due to the fact that our mind is racing ahead to what we're going to say, rather than really listening. So use a trick or two to remember names. Repeat it, such as "Sally, I am pleased to meet you;" or "is that Steven with a "V"?

As the conversation moves forward, try to balance talking with listening. Remember, most people love to talk about themselves, so if you are shy ask open ended questions, not questions that can be answered with a yes or no. Then listen. Be interested in the other person.

Resist the urge to talk about yourself and your accomplishments. Author John Maxwell said "People don't care how much you know, until they know how much you care." Stephen Hawkins said "People who boast about their I.Q. are losers." Instead, focus on the other person. You will be amazed at what you will learn!

"No one ever listened his way out of a job"—President Calvin Coolidge

Cell phones
at the office >

It seems we haven't really progressed
very far in our cell phone etiquette;
a lot of rules continue to be broken.

During a meeting I attended a participant's cell phone rang. It had a silly, annoying ring tone, and to make matters worse, she couldn't find the offending object in her large handbag. The person giving the report stopped talking, and the rest of us sat in awkward silence, while our embarrassed colleague rummaged. I'm not unsympathetic here because, honestly, that has happened to most of us.

The Director of the Information Center at the Society for Human Resource Management, Rebecca Hastings said, "Right now, cell phones are the cigarettes of this decade," adding "It's an addiction." Well, let's face it. She is right.

Here are some generally accepted rules of cell phone etiquette in the office:

- At your desk, turn off your cell phone or set it to "vibrate." Unless your cell phone is company-issued for business use, set your unit to vibrate. Even if you've selected a tasteful ring tone, repetitive incoming calls will be noticed (negatively) by co-workers and management.

- Let personal calls go to voicemail. Frequent personal calls during your workday can reflect adversely on your professional reputation.

- When you must use your cell phone, find a private, quiet place to make your calls. Observe the "ten foot rule." Make every effort to respect co-workers spaces.

- Don't bring your cell phone to meetings. I know these are fighting words to some, but neglecting this one rule can hurt your career. If an important call is expected, either for business or a family emergency, and you absolutely have to have your cell phone, use the "vibrate" mode.

- Don't use your cell phone in restrooms. Why? You may not know who else may be using the facilities who could overhear private or sensitive issues. There are well-documented stories of confidential information falling into the wrong hands just from violating this seemingly innocent rule.

- Eliminate unprofessional ring tones. Either keep your cell phone on vibrate at all times at work or change to a more professional ring tone during your work day.

- Please, no loud conversations! Sometimes called "holding court," it is just plain annoying to others.

- Use text messages instead of voice calls to maintain professionalism. If you have to have a personal communication, send a text message. It's quick and, more important, silent.

Remember, you are in charge of your professional image. Don't let poor cell phone etiquette impair your career.

Great conversations >

The art of conversation
begins with conversational etiquette.

Have you ever been in the company of a person who was a thoroughly engaging conversationalist? I'm not talking about a good public or motivational speaker, but of one with whom it is a pleasure to engage in conversation. From Socrates to Winston Churchill, and more recently to Christopher Hitchens, brilliant conversationalists engage with and encourage others to discuss ideas. They are ones who will leave you stimulated, energized, and animated.

George Orwell, in 1946, grumbled, "In very many English homes the radio is literally never turned off. ... The music prevents the conversation from becoming serious or even coherent." Later television was similarly blamed. Stephen Miller in his book *Conversation: A History of a Declining Art* noted that "neither digital music players nor computers were invented to help people avoid real conversation, but they have that effect."

Check out bookstores and you will find a surprising number of books on how to be a better conversationalist. These books, and the advice they contain, are not a modern phenomenon, as the hints and tips found in them go back hundreds of years.

According to research by the State University of New York at New Paltz, interrupting another is one of the ten acts of rudeness in the workplace. That principle goes back to Cicero, who wrote in 44BC "...speak clearly; speak easily but not too much, especially when others want their turn; do not interrupt; be courteous; deal seriously with serious matters and gracefully with lighter ones; never criticize people behind their backs; stick to subjects of general interest; do not talk about yourself; and, above all, never lose your temper."

Self- help gurus have been giving similar advice ever since. Cicero didn't mention that it was important to remember names and listen carefully to what others are saying. However, Dale Carnegie picked that up in his book *How to Win Friends and Influence People*.

In the late 17th Century the French nobility required the scintillating conversationalist to have "good manners, wit, gallantry, obligingness, cheerfulness and flattery." These qualities are still helpful in our social and professional lives, although "flattery" strikes us as insincere today.

Coming closer to our age, Margaret Shepherd, author of *The Art of Civilized Conversation: A guide to Expressing Yourself, with Style and Grace*, admonishes us not to speak longer than four minutes without interruption. (That's a little long, don't you think?) She also advised "if your dinner plate is full when others are finished... stop talking!" So this writer will stop here!

Conversation is food for the soul—Proverb

Fear of
public speaking >

Never forget public speaking
is about the "public" you're
addressing; be prepared, but focus
on your audience.

I watched a movie called The King's Speech. The beginning of this true story chronicled the worst kind of fear that public speaking conjures up. The Duke of York, soon to be King of England, suffered from an incapacitating stammer, and thousands of people were eagerly anticipating his radio speech, but nothing came out of his mouth.

Now most of us will never experience that kind of crippling anxiety, although some actors dream that very nightmare. About three fourths of us suffer from some sort of fear of public speaking or stage fright. Research reveals that this phobia is the number one fear or dread that humans experience – even more frightening than the thought of death!

Public speaking anxiety can delay a college graduation; hinder a career, and impact salaries and promotions. We might not be able to eliminate nervousness entirely, but there are ways to overcome anxiety, increase confidence, and ease the dread that is hindering a gratifying and worthwhile experience.

Keep in mind that nerves are not your enemy. This natural response can be used to energize your speech. For instance, some presenters and performers worry if they don't get nervous, feeling that will take the "edge" off of their performance.

The Scouts motto "Be Prepared" applies here. Author Amit Kalantri said "Preparation doesn't assure victory, it assures confidence." So prepare your speech well in advance; practice, practice, and practice again. After all, isn't that what all great performers do—whether acting, singing, playing music or playing sports? In your practice, find the places to pause, to look up, and to relate to your audience. The mark of a nervous, ill-prepared speaker is revealed when a speech is rattled off without pause or nuance.

You might consider saying less about your topic, but saying it well. After all, one doesn't often hear complaints that a speech wasn't long enough. I must warn you, though, saying less, like writing less, takes longer to prepare.

The old adage "fake it until you make it" works well here. When stepping to the podium assume a strong posture, with head up, shoulders back, looking up, not down, and breathe deeply. Relax your face and smile. Research shows that using these simple techniques can change the body's chemistry, and help us calm down.

Finally, enjoy the experience! Yes, everyone is looking at you, but think if no one was interested in you or your topic. As speakers, it is our obligation to focus on our audience, rather than ourselves.

P.S. And yes, King George VI did overcome his debilitating speech impediment.

Phubbing –
eh, what? >

"Smart" phones can be used
in such "dumb" ways during real-time
social interactions.

Phubbing? What on earth is phubbing? I must admit that was my initial reaction when I recently read about the phenomena in a post in Debrett's, the venerable English etiquette authority. I felt a little out of touch because I had never heard the word before. It turns out it was generated through research by language and marketing experts at the University of Sydney in 2012. It is now a bona fide word in many dictionaries.

What does this funny sounding word mean? It is a combination of "phone" and "snubbing" and it means ignoring someone while interacting with one's smart device. Who knew? Certainly not me, and I bet you millennials are having a snicker at my expense right now!

Who knew that the word would go viral, and that a graduate student in Australia started a "Stop Phubbing" campaign to address this growing social problem? He even suggested (tongue in cheek, perhaps) staging interventions as a possible solution. The campaign spread around the world and attracted over 300 million people, encouraging dialogues on smart phone etiquette.

It's fun to say the word phubbing. Let's face it, though, it's not exactly fun to be phubbed, as all of us have surely been. We had better come clean here too, and admit that most of us have been guilty of being the phubber. How often have you felt annoyed or even hurt and marginalized when a friend, relative, or co-worker ignored you in favor of their smart device? This is phubbing and, at its worst, it is breaking up relationships both personal and professional.

Some feel that this 21st century phenomenon is simply part of modern life, and that it's harmless. But let's look at what research says about the effects of phubbing. Emma Seppala, a psychologist at Stanford and Yale universities, and author of *The Happiness Track* observes "… phubbing is meant to connect you with someone through social media or texting…but it actually can severely disrupt your present-moment, in-person relationships."

Studies show that phubbing actually makes one feel less connected, and that being phubbed negatively impacts inclusiveness, self-esteem, and other fundamental needs by making persons feel left out or ostracized. I must say, though, that one doesn't really need a scientific study to conclude that people's feelings get hurt if they are snubbed!

I think we can all agree that phubbing isn't really good for anyone. Now that we have a name for it, let's consider cutting back on this demeaning habit. Let's face it—phubbing is just plain rude!

It's rude to interrupt >

Many of us have a propensity
for this annoying habit; here's why.

Well, we all know that! We've been told since childhood that it's rude to interrupt, yet still we do it. Joel H. Neuman, director of the Center for Applied Management at the State University of New York at New Paltz, developed a list of the most commonly cited aggressive behaviors in the workplace and "interrupting others when they are speaking or working" was number two on the list.

In my Business Etiquette seminars I advise clients not to interrupt two people that are deep in conversation. Yet that happens all the time. Recently I observed an intense conversation between two people that was interrupted by another, who barged into their space. The interrupter didn't even acknowledge one person, and in fact turned his back on him. Was that irritating? You bet it was! A situation like that reminds us to adhere to Emily Post's advice that "it is easy to be pleasant when things are going well, but better call up our automatic (practiced!) good manners when things become unpleasant."

Although this sort of behavior has become routine, it is still as rude as it has always been. So why do many people constantly interrupt conversations, pop into offices uninvited, and send a barrage of texts, tweets, and social media alerts? It seems we humans have a propensity for this annoying habit.

Some famous observations on interrupting:

"People who say it cannot be done should not interrupt those who are doing it," said writer George Bernard Shaw.

Winston Churchill fumed "Don't interrupt me while I'm interrupting."

Napoleon Bonaparte advised "Never interrupt your enemy when he is making a mistake." This could also be good business advice, albeit a little harsh.

Since interrupting will not advance one's career; why we do it? Here are some reasons:

- Lack of self-awareness: Not realizing you are interrupting others.
- Fear of forgetting what you want to say, and not actively listening.
- Need to prove expertize.
- Interrupting is pervasive behavior in your office or family.
- You can't wait to get your point across because you're passionate about the subject matter.

Do recognize however that if the interrupter is senior to you, it's best to stop talking and let the conversation take its course. If a person consistently interrupts you, and is not your senior, you can hold up your hand and say, "Just a second, I'm not finished," in a pleasant tone and you might even add a smile.

Oh, and lest I be tagged a goody-goody, let me readily admit that I am far from perfectly polite in this department. Just ask my family!

A FEW MORE ETIQUETTE MATTERS

A world of thanks
('No problem') >

Expressing appreciation is a good thing
and it is important to do it properly.

Just about every country in the world has an expression for gratitude or thanks. Whether it is "thank you" in English speaking countries, "arigato" in Japan, "danke" in Germany, "grazie" in Italy, or "merci beaucoup" in France, expressions of gratitude are spoken millions of times a day, in hundreds of countries throughout the world. Let's consider the response to a "thank you!" How do you reply when someone thanks you?

When people thank you, they are acknowledging you, and giving you and your contribution significance and value. How you acknowledge that is important. Do you accept the praise in a gracious manner, or do you in some way shrug it off, and dismiss it as somehow not being deserving of praise. "Oh, I'm just doing my job," "it was nothing," or "forget It."

If you think about it, handling a "thank you" message in that way somehow diminishes the message, and even diminishes the person offering the gratitude. My least favorite response to "Thank you!" is "No problem."

I train waiters in high-end restaurants and country clubs on proper dining service. I advise the staff members not to say "no problem" when a guest thanks them. People who say "no problem" in reply to "thank you," are basically saying that there was a problem, but that they have overlooked it. Not appropriate at all.

In England, Canada and some parts of Europe, one often hears, "Don't mention it," or "Not at all," or the more formal, "My pleasure." In the U.S. the response to a compliment or a thank you is simply, "You're welcome."

Moving to the other side of this topic: do you genuinely and readily give praise, and thank colleagues? Do you acknowledge good work or outstanding contributions made by members of your team? Sometimes we fail to recognize that readily expressing our appreciation can mean a great deal to another person.

There are some professionals who think that doing good work has its own reward, and that persons should not be thanked or acknowledged for something that they are paid to do. May I suggest that that thinking is dinosaurian. Studies show that humans thrive under positive feedback and approbation.

Look for ways to showcase the work of colleagues or other professionals. Share their positive contributions with others. Many of us bloom when we are praised and thanked. So thank frequently, praise often, and when thanks come your way, remember to respond graciously.

The rules
for volunteering >

Being a volunteer can be enormously
fulfilling. If you abide by these rules
your chances of success are improved
greatly.

Most of us have extraordinary demands on our time: children, challenging jobs, travel schedules, church, and civic responsibilities. There's an expression, "If you want something done, find a busy person to do it."

Volunteering helps professionals make contacts that make them visible in their community, which in turn, can advance careers. Volunteering helps develop compassion towards those who are less fortunate. There is an enormous sense of satisfaction that comes in helping people or organizations that need assistance.

Volunteering can be a lot of fun, too. It can open doors we've always wanted to go through. Volunteer for a cause that makes you happy. It may or may not be in your field. Choose something that gives you satisfaction.

I remember a successful construction company owner who volunteered his time with a community theatre. When asked to build sets, he replied, "I'm a builder by day, I want to be an actor by night." He made a fine actor in the local community theatre for many years. The added bonus for the acting company was that, when it needed money or materials, our builder/actor was the first to open his wallet. He said that being a part of the group gave him great pleasure, and that he always got back much more than he gave.

Tips for volunteer board members:

- Treat your commitment seriously.
- Always attend scheduled meetings.
- Do your homework.
- Arrive on time and stay until the end.
  Staying for a few minutes and then dashing off is simply bad form.
- Listen to and be responsive to the paid staff.
- Keep an eye out for future board members:
  new blood invigorates an organization.
- Be up front about what you can and cannot do financially.
  Taking on board responsibilities often includes the expectation
  of a financial contribution.
- Boards need contributors, and also need talented, energetic, members.

Tips for fundraiser organizers:

- Obtaining speakers doesn't stop at getting a "yes."
- If you are responsible for obtaining a speaker for an event,
  once someone agrees to volunteer his/her expertise and time
  to speak at your event, you must treat him/her like gold.
- Make sure he/she knows exactly the name, purpose, time, and place of the event.
- Confirm and reconfirm.
- Be there to greet your speakers, and introduce them to key people.

Civility in today's world >

Our society is increasingly
diminishing the role of civility
in our daily lives and it's time we
reclaim this essence of civilization.

We hear a lot about Civility and of the lack thereof these days, but what exactly is it? The Institute for Civility in Government, a non-profit, non-partisan organization, explains it this way: "Civility is about more than just politeness, although politeness is a necessary first step. It is about disagreeing without disrespect…Civility is the hard work of staying present even with those with whom we have deep-rooted and fierce disagreements." That definition could certainly apply to us in our professional and social life too!

We hear increasingly alarming stories of incivility in today's world. Flaming emails, incendiary blog comments, cyber bullying, rancorous television discussions, mean spirited political debates, sullen children grunting at parents and teachers, and getting away with it! The list is endless, and we haven't even touched road rage!

According to a survey conducted by Weber Shandwick and Powell Tate, in partnership with KRC Research "…an overwhelming majority of Americans view the erosion of civility in human interaction today as a major problem …" and "…The tone of incivility is causing Americans to tune out from the most fundamental elements of our democracy — government and politics, news coverage and reporting, and opinion pieces and editorials in newspapers and magazines…." Well, that's disheartening, wouldn't you agree?

Faced with this lack of civility, some people are taking direct action. We hear of some deciding not to do business with a company again, cancelling subscriptions to newspapers or magazines, and not watching, or listening to, some radio or television shows. Because of a certain anonymity and lack of accountability, social networks have become the breeding grounds for some pretty upsetting examples of incivility. I have a friend who recently announced to all his "friends" on an online social site that, because of the tone of rancor and rudeness that some of the posts were taking, he was no longer going to participate.

What to do about this alarming trend of incivility that permeates our society? I think we can all agree that civility starts in the home. Hard as the challenge sometimes can be, parents need to take back the reigns and refuse to accept rude behavior from their children. Social networks, a vast resource for communication and business, would do well to consider methods of making their sites safer and more civil.

CEO's are the mentors and models for setting the tone for civility in the work place. They should not tolerate rude and uncivil behavior from their executives or their staff. Their customer service interface is bound to be contaminated, and the shrewd business person realizes that uncivil customer service always results in lost profits. Ultimately, to stem the erosion of civility, we may have to rely on the marketplace's strongest motivator – the profit motive!

Some (unfortunately) forgotten rules >

Etiquette and good taste
never go out of style.

Did you know that the first book of etiquette was written on papyrus in Egypt around 2000 B.C. by a man called Ptahhotep? The astonishing thing about this is that this papyrus is still preserved in the Bibliotheque Nationale in Paris, and is called the Prisse Papyrus. It is interesting to reflect that, over the eons, people have tried to codify the rules of proper behavior. Considering what is going on in the world today, we're not doing too great a job of it, but still we try!

Etiquette used to be considered the glue that bound society together. It helped family, friends, neighbors and colleagues to interact without causing offense, and hence, bad feelings. Many of these rules are disappearing in a world where such things are considered archaic and unnecessary. . Here are some of them, though, that might assist you, especially the professional you, to negotiate your way in society today.

- Never borrow or discuss money, or brag about your possessions and their cost.
- Do not name drop, "When I was having dinner with Lady Spendsalot..."
- Use discretion on the street—don't do anything to call attention to yourself.
- Do arrive on time—really, there's no such thing as "fashionably late."
- Do leave on time—not too early, not too late, and not too tipsy!!!
- Never leave before the guest of honor leaves.
- The previous rule is almost completely ignored today, but at least be aware of it.
  Take as your model the bride and groom, the governor, the President
  of the United States!
- Never ask for gifts. Oh, yes, I do include the gift registry here!
  That "option" is synonymous to asking for gifts.
- Don't forget your "thank you" note! Teach the children to write them, too.

And finally, a little lecture...

In days gone by, a man would always open a door for a woman. My son, (a career military officer) always opens car doors for his mother, his wife and his little daughter, and we love it! Some business women can take offense by this gesture. My advice to women in this situation is not to confuse good manners with chauvinism. Allow the door to be opened if offered, and enjoy the moment!

Money matters >

Friends and associates may not
call you on it, but if you display a
tactless approach to money matters,
they are probably talking to
each other about it.

Let's talk about the etiquette of money. In Victorian times it was very poor form indeed to talk about money and many, including yours truly, retain that attitude. Those who talk about their finances or brag that they are anything but "comfortable" are not well received in some circles.

A little restraint is in order. We need to show some basic common courtesy when it comes to money. Do you know the person who refuses to leave a decent tip, or the one who constantly brags about how much they earn, or how much they pay for clothes, cars, vacations? All of the above are financial *faux pas*, or social blunders. It's from the French and means false step. The opposite of putting your best foot forward!

Here are some money etiquette mistakes that we should avoid both in our business and social lives.

- Being a skimpy tipper. Here's a tip on that: servers earn very little money, and rely on tips for their income. As of 2011, the federal minimum wage for wait staff was $2.13 per hour plus tips, and the general federal minimum wage rate was $7.25. Unless your waiter snarled at you, or deliberately dropped spaghetti in your lap, please tip 15–20%, and really, err on the side of 20%.

- Talking about how much money you earn. Taking every opportunity to share one's affluence just makes one look like a showoff, and no one likes a braggart.

- Similarly, talking about how much you paid for items, be it jewelry, clothes, cars and even houses is a no-no.

- Not re-paying hospitality. We all have them: the friends or associates who always accept your invitation, but never reciprocate. That usually ends up with those people being ostracized, and not included in events.

- Offering unreasonable proposals when negotiating. Be very careful here. The fastest way to end a negotiation is to make a ludicrously low offer. It indicates that you aren't serious, and it can be very insulting. Do your homework, find out the true value of things, and never make your opening offer too low. This rule becomes even more important in the international business arena.

- Mixing business with friendship. .Always dicey and usually ends badly.

- And need I say it? Asking for or lending money to friends, relatives, or associates. It usually ends badly for both parties. If you have some extra money, it's best to give it, rather than lend it. You'll feel good about it!

Tips on tipping >

You want service staff to remember you for the right reasons, and tipping correctly is the best way to make sure they do.

I have mentioned tipping previously, and it occurred to me that we might want to further examine this practice, which often makes people very nervous. Whom do I tip? How much do I tip? What if I'm travelling?

There are several theories on how tips originated. An appealing tale goes back to the eighteenth century writer Dr. Johnson and his companion, Mr. Boswell. It is told, at their public house, they began throwing a few pennies in a box labeled "To Insure Promptness" (T.I.P.) An old-fashioned tip jar to encourage better service!

The concept arrived in Colonial America from England, but after the revolution it was considered a relic of the British class system. Only social inferiors were tipped, and that notion was not supposed to exist in the new world. That attitude changed quickly, and tipping returned with as much vigor as today.

These days wait persons, cab drivers, hairdresser and all sorts of "service" professionals rely on tips as part of their income. The addition of a gratuity or tip is now thought of as a gift for good service. However, it is still a source of confusion and stress for many people.

Here are some tips on tipping in the United States:

- Some restaurants automatically charge a gratuity for large parties, so check the bill.
- Maitre d'—no need to tip unless he goes above and beyond to seat you on a busy night. Then $10–$20.
- Sommelier or Wine Steward—tip separately—15%, but ask your server if the sommelier is already being tipped based on wine sales.
- Wait Staff—do try to leave 20%. (Please overtip breakfast wait staff!)
     Buffet—10%.
     Barista—10%.
     Drinks served at a bar—$1–$2 per drink or 15% of the bill.
- Home Delivery of Food—$2–$5 or 10–15% of the bill.
- Porters—$2 per bag—I tend to up that—porters are invaluable!
- Doormen—$1–$5 depending on the quality of the hotel.
- Bellhops—$2–$3 per bag.
- Hotel Maids—$2–$5 per night. (Please don't forget the hotel maid!)
- Taxi Drivers—15–20%.
- Valet Attendants—$2–$5 dollars when car is returned.
- Hairstylists or Barbers—15–20% percent.*
- Manicurists—15–20%.*
     *Not tipping the owner is old etiquette.

All that said, if you are a generous tipper, you will be remembered and treated very well! And that's the point, right?

Kindness
in the workplace >

Good behavior in the workplace
is more than not eating someone
else's food from the refrigerator...
a lot more.

Plato, the Greek philosopher, was a mathematician, a student of Socrates, a writer of philosophical dialogues, and founder of the Academy in Athens, the first institution of higher learning in the Western world. He wrote "Be kind, for everyone you meet is fighting a hard battle."

In the business arena, as in every other walk of life, people can grow alienated from one another. The root cause might be cultural, it might be competitiveness between organizations and teams within organizations, or it might be an ongoing disagreement between a supervisor and a direct report.

Etiquette, whether in a business or social setting, is a set of rules governing behavior that is regarded as correct and accepted. Let's take a look at a few simple guidelines that we could practice to help promote a sense of civility and manners in the workplace, or, in other words, kindness.

- Agree to Disagree.
  Yes, we know the U.S. Constitution guarantees us freedom of speech, but there are limits, and our own sense of courtesy should take over. We should always try to conduct business conversation in a respectful manner. So, if you can't agree, then agree to disagree!

- Stick with the facts, please, just the facts.
  A professional discussion should stick to the facts. Try to understand the other person's point. Never, never launch an 'ad hominem' (personal) attack upon another person. It is fine to dispute another's point, but not in a nasty, unpleasant manner.

- Remain calm.
  The calm, unruffled person always looks confident and in control. "Keep Calm and Carry On." That saying came from the British during World War II. When England (especially London) was being repeatedly bombed, the British people calmly went about their business to the admiration of the free world. We might remember that when we find ourselves in an infuriating situation.

- Yelling and Shouting is not professional.
  Raising your voice to another signals that you are being unsuitably emotional, out of control or, perhaps, unstable. That behavior will never move you up the rungs of the professional ladder.

Plato's words resonate even today. Even those who appear to be the most successful and happy carry a burden. Everyone has some worries—be it a medical situation, worry about a child, a teenager, an elderly parent, or a financial issue. The list is endless. None of us is exempt from the burden of living – so let's be kind to our fellow travelers on the journey of life!

George says >

Think 18th Century etiquette rules would be antiquated and no longer apropos? Think again.

Based on the *Exercise of a Schoolboy**

Can you imagine a young boy of less than sixteen laboring to transcribe one hundred and ten etiquette rules from a French etiquette book? I hope you are as captivated as I was to read just a select baker's dozen. I know you will agree that, although the "spelling" and style are amusing to our modern sensibilities, the message remains [forgive my bracketed comments!]. Oh, the boy was George Washington!

1. Every Action done in Company, ought to be with Some Sign of Respect, to those that are Present. [Public prayer debate?]
2. When in Company, put not your Hands to any Part of the Body, not usualy Discovered. [Oh, my!]
3. Show Nothing to your Friend that may affright him. [How about a selfy?]
4. In the Presence of Others Sing not to yourself with a humming Noise, nor Drum with your Fingers or Feet. [Unless plugged into an itune?]
5. Gentlemen lay with their things on the floor, not within a pile of like family members. [Clean up your room!]
6. If You Cough, Sneeze, Sigh, or Yawn, do it not Loud but Privately; and Speak not in your Yawning, but put Your handkercheif or Hand before your face and turn aside. [Into your elbow!]
7. Sleep not when others Speak, Sit not when others stand, Speak not when you Should hold your Peace, walk not on when others Stop. [What a wonderful world it would be!]
8. Put not off your Cloths in the presence of Others, nor go out your Chamber half Drest. [Pajama bottoms? Really!]
9. At Play and at Fire it's Good manners to Give Place to the last Commer, and affect not to Speak Louder than Ordinary. [Too bad! I got here first.]
10. When you Sit down, Keep your Feet firm and Even, without putting one on the other or Crossing them. [Showing the sole of your foot is offensive in some cultures today!]
11. Read no Letters, Books, or Papers [or iphones!] in Company but when there is a Necessity for the doing of it you must ask leave …
12. Let your Discourse with Men of Business be Short and Comprehensive. [Oh, don't we wish?]
13. In visiting the Sick, do not Presently play the Physicion if you be not Knowing therein. [Tell that to your hypochondriacal friends!]

*Washington, George. *Rules of Civility & Decent Behaviour in Company and Conversation: a Book of Etiquette.* Williamsburg, VA: Beaver Press, 1971.

Politics
equals incivility? >

Talking politics can quickly escalate
to bad form in social settings.

Some of you will read this before November 4 when elections will be held for the U.S. Senate, the U.S. House of Representatives, some governorships, and some local political offices. The nasty accusations and fingerpointings are already flying!

Every day we hear the pundits and the press lamenting about incivilty in politics while often fuelling the fire themselves. Yet this is not a new phenomenon. In England, politicians traditionally applaud each other in the House of Commons for their loud quarrels. Winston Churchill's invective was legendary, but he was saved by his wit—something, it seems, in short supply today. Closer to home, John Adams and Thomas Jefferson's animosity and conflicts were renowned—so much so that John Adams's last words on his death bed were "Thomas Jefferson survives."

James H. Mullen, President of Allegheny College, which gives an annual award called Prize for Civility in Public Life, wrote "… national surveys confirm what we all suspect—that perceptions of political civility are down and declining. These perceptions are having a negative effect on political participation, particularly among the generation that will inherit our democracy." President Mullen worried that "… incivility will cause fewer and fewer young people to seek a career in public service… we are at risk of losing an entire generation to public service -- with potentially catastrophic consequences."

Let's bring it to a more personal level. I was at a social gathering when one of the guests, during a conversation about college tuitions, pronounced "I could never be friends with a (here fill in the political party.) I was, I admit, shocked. Obviously this woman had never heard of the adage that politics and religion are taboo at social gatherings. And really that's not completely accurate. The guest assumed that all in the room were of like minds. I advise participants in my business etiquette seminars to avoid bringing up politics or religion. It's just not worth the risk these days!

It's great to have a spirited debate. My husband has a friend of over 25 years, and they are extreme opposites when it comes to politics. Yet they have maintained a steadfast friendship, as they debate their opposing views with wit, warmth—and civility!

So let's stop the snide remarks, the sneers, the invective when it comes to politics. Count to ten and, with a smile, change the subject. My favorite way is to murmur a quote from Noel Coward, "Isn't it nice we're having weather!" That definitely halts the conversation, and invariably brings a smile!

Picking up the tab >

When it comes to paying the bill
at a meal where business happens,
there should be no confusion—
especially when clarified up front.

It's no secret that taking an associate or client for a meal is a successful way to increase your business. Much of the world's business is conducted (or decided) during meals. They are great opportunities to start new relationships and/or strengthen existing ones.

So who pays the bill? Who picks up that check? There's nothing complicated about this: if you do the inviting, you do the paying. I heard from a colleague recently who was baffled by the following scenario. He was invited by businessmen to lunch, the purpose of which was solicitation. In other words, those doing the inviting were requesting help in promoting their business. After the meal the waitress asked "separate checks or together?" After an awkward pause, my colleague said "I'll get mine."

In business, it is a given that if you invite someone to lunch or dinner to discuss business you should always expect to pay. Failing to do that can, and usually will, ruin a business transaction.

When a businesswoman hosts a male client, it can become problematical if the man is uncomfortable with a woman picking up the check. Often I make it clear to the staff at the beginning of the meal that the check will come to me. Or I prearrange payment. I arrive early, give my credit card to the appropriate person, tell them the gratuity I wish to add, and receive the processed bill when I leave. Caution: that tactic is not as easy as it used to be because of portable payment methods at the table, not to mention the rise of credit card fraud.

When all is said and done, though, the best way to handle the bill for a business meal is to use the words "…be my guest" ahead of time, as in, "Let's meet for dinner to discuss this topic, and of course you will be my guest."

There are always exceptions to most rules. Some companies and governmental agencies have strict policies against gifts, including meals. In that case, just ask the server to divide the costs. Sometimes people who meet regularly for a meal agree to go 50/50. That usually works well. The important thing in all of this is to make the arrangements, and your intentions, very clear ahead of time. All of this is black and white. There are no gray areas unless we create them!

Team player >

If you're not a team player,
you might need to rethink that
position if you work with others.

In the corporate world today it is generally accepted that being a team player is key to one's professional success. Some of us have team playing in our DNA. Others of us have learned it through experience. Some of us just plain don't want to be, and won't ever be, a team player! That's quite all right. Many professions need the lone player. Some Information Technology jobs, for instance, come readily to mind. However, no matter what your position, thoughtfulness and good manners will make you a more valuable asset to any organization.

When my husband retired from a senior position at a major university, many people came to him to wish him well. He was gratified that so many came from the bottom rung of the institution. Why was this? He always treated them with respect and courtesy: in other words, he gave them value. The serendipitous result was that he could always get things done, because while he respected them, they returned his kindness with loyalty. He was courteous to absolutely everyone, from the President to the housekeeping staff.

Being a good team player helps win the respect of your co-workers, so let's look at some ways to improve teamwork:

- Always be loyal to your boss and organization, especially outside the office. Remember the old adage: we can criticize our family, but not to strangers!
- Be as courteous to those on the bottom of the job scale as to your boss.
- Don't carry tales—unless the person involved is dealing drugs!
- Be kind to newcomers: make them feel welcome and a part of the team.
- Follow the Golden Rule: treat everyone as you would like to be treated.
- Keep your word: say what you will do, and then do it.
- Work on honing your sense of humor and learn to laugh at yourself.
- Take responsibility for your errors. We're human and we make mistakes.
- When one is genuinely kind and courteous, it improves office morale. Good work is done in a pleasant atmosphere.
- Curtail your urge to gossip: gossiping can derail your career.
- Give credit where credit is due.
- Be inclusive! Why not say, "We did that!" rather than, "I did that!"?

Vince Lombardi summed it up nicely when he said, "Individual commitment to a group effort—that is what makes a team work, a company work, a society work, a civilization work."

Are we nice, kind or weak? >

One of the three adjectives used
to describe polite people is a better
application than the other two.

As you know, I am an etiquette and protocol professional. Hence by my instincts and training I tend to be a nice or kind person. Sometimes my niceness or kindness is taken for weakness. That is not a good idea at all, by the way! Let's examine these three words— nice, kind and weak – and see how they apply to us in both our personal and professional lives.

The word "nice" has its roots in the Latin nescuis meaning "ignorant" and "unaware," and the 12th century Old French nice meaning "weak, needy, simple, silly, foolish." It then progressed to "fussy, fastidious" and "dainty, delicate" in the 14the century to "agreeable, delightful" in the 1700's.

The word "kind" is from the Old English gecynde and had to do with "the feelings of relatives for each other." It progressed to "well-disposed and benign, compassionate" around the 13th century.

The word "weak" is found in Old Norse and Old English around the 13th Century, with meanings of "weak, soft, compliant", and evolving into a sense of "lacking authority" in the 15th century.

We can already see a difference in the meanings of "nice" and "kind." While today they are definitely close, they don't really belong together. "Nice" and "weak" are better paired.

According to some experts, a nice person is a people pleaser, a person who wants others to like him or her at all costs. This person is careful not to disagree with others. In meetings, for example, a 'nice' person would prefer to avoid conflict. The nice person has a very hard time saying "no" and often overcommits to others. He or she will do favors for persons in authority, hoping to get approval, and emotional needs fulfilled. They are operating from an anxious need to be accepted and liked. Unfortunately, I think we could easily substitute the word "weak" here.

On the other hand, a kind person is one who truly cares about people, is "nice" to others, but does not back away from stating what they think in order to avoid conflict. The kind person operates from a position of empathy. The kind person has no trouble saying "no", and does not allow others to manipulate him or her. The kind person functions without any expectation of reward or return.

So let's give some thought as to what sort of persons we are in our personal and professional relationships. Are we kind rather than nice to our colleagues and friends? Are we kind rather than nice to our children, and our families? Something to consider, don't you think?

Based on
Exercise of a
Schoolboy >

A 15-year old shows a pretty good
understanding of manners; perhaps
presidential candidates should take
note.

Previously, we considered some of the one hundred and ten etiquette rules that George Washington, while not quite sixteen years old, transcribed from a French etiquette book. Here are more, and as in the earlier column, I've kept the original "spelling" and style and again, couldn't resist a comment or two!

1. If You Cough, Sneeze, Sigh, or Yawn, do it not Loud but Privately; and Speak not in your Yawning, but put Your handkercheif or Hand before your face and turn aside. [Mother always said, "Cover your mouth!"]
2. Jog not the Table or Desk on which Another reads or writes, lean not upon any one. [Respect another's space.]
3. Read no Letters, Books, or Papers in Company but when there is a Necessity for the doing of it you must ask leave... [What about emails and texts?]
4. A Man ought not to value himself of his Atchievements, or rare Qualities of wit; much less of his riches Virtue or Kindred. [Don't brag about yourself!]
5. If any one come to Speak to you while you are Sitting Stand up tho he be your Inferiour...[Standing shows respect.]
6. In writing or Speaking, give to every Person his due Title According to his Degree & the Custom of the Place. [Precedence and honorifics are still important, whether with diplomats or business persons.]
7. Mock not nor Jest at any thing of Importance break no Jest that are Sharp Biting and if you Deliver any thing witty and Pleasent abstain from Laughing there at yourself. [Laughing at your own jokes!]
8. Be not hasty to believe flying Reports to the Disparagement of any. [Or those pesky, unwanted rants in emails, tweets, and texts.]
9. In your Apparel be Modest and endeavour to accomodate Nature...[Oh my, yes!]
10. Associate yourself with Men of good Quality if you Esteem your own Reputation; for 'tis better to be alone than in bad Company. ["If you choose bad companions, no one will believe that you are anything but bad yourself." Aesop and your mother!]
11. Speak not of doleful Things in a Time of Mirth or at the Table; Speak not of Melancholy Things as Death and Wounds, and if others Mention them Change if you can the Discourse... [Forgo your health and medical history.]
12. Speak not injurious Words neither in Jest nor Earnest... [nor on Social Media.]

*Washington, George. *Rules of Civility & Decent Behaviour in Company and Conversation: a Book of Etiquette.* Williamsburg, VA: Beaver Press, 1971.

Can kindness be taught? Is rudeness contagious? >

Too often these days niceties are disregarded; we should teach kindness.

At the end of my etiquette seminars I introduce the following quote from Plato: "Be kind, for everyone you meet is fighting a hard battle." Plato was a philosopher in Classical Greece, a mathematician, a student of Socrates, a writer of philosophical dialogues, and founder of the Academy in Athens, the first institution of higher learning in the Western world.

Usually I get puzzled looks. Then thoughtful nods as I advance the notion that everyone in the room, including me, carries some sort of burden. The burden might be about finances, health, personal relationships, grades, worry about a child or an elderly parent—the list can be endless. It is the human condition to carry some sort of burden.

What about rudeness to each other? In the 1960's a Stanford University professor posited "the broken window theory" which suggested that small crimes in neighborhoods, like breaking windows and leaving garbage unattended, if ignored, becomes contagious, worsens, and leads to more serious crimes. (Note: this theory does have its critics.)

The same theory could be applied to rudeness. We were taught as children to say "please" and" thank you", to hold the door for the next person, and to give up our seats to an adult. Too often these days the niceties are being disregarded. We neglect the little phrases and gestures that make life more pleasing and agreeable. Perhaps this is not deliberate behavior; but rather thoughtlessness or indifference.

Whatever the reason, according to the study above, "Being on the receiving end of rude behavior wears people down...and depletes the resources they have for controlling their own behavior." ..."The result makes you impatient at home, bristly at work, and infects those around you to do the same."

So can kindness be taught in school? Some have questions on whether on not personality traits such as kindness can be taught like French or Geography. Some (like this writer) think that kindness begins in the home, but that maybe it can be extended to the schoolroom.

There is a Kindness Curriculum at the Center for Healthy Minds at the University of Wisconsin, Madison. This is part of a growing movement that teaches kindness, empathy and emotional intelligence in schools. This all suggests that the next time we feel slighted by someone's behavior or lack thereof, think of that long ago quote from Plato, and let's give each other a break. Ah yes! The Golden Rule!

Be kind whenever possible. It is always possible.—Dalai Lama

Your Etiquette Quiz

Here's a fun little quiz completely based on the advice and ideas shared in this book. (That's right, readers...all the answers are right here in the book!)

1. **The best time to share your dietary restrictions with a host is:**
   A   before you attend, when you accept the invitation
   B   at mealtime (so no one had to prepare anything special;
       you don't have to partake or you consume only what you are able)
   C   never; it is rude to expect special provisions

2. **A man can leave his hat on inside a post office**
   TRUE
   FALSE

3. **There should be no differences between how a man and woman shakes hands**
   TRUE
   FALSE

4. **It is acceptable to remove an oyster from its shell with your finger**
   TRUE
   FALSE

5. **An RSVP:**
   A   requires a response if you are not able to attend
   B   requires a response if you are able to attend
   C   requires a response whether or not you are attending

6. **Direct eye contact during a conversation varies depending on cultural norms; however, in American business engagements, direct eye contact is:**
   A   ideal; the more—the better
   B   considered intrusive or an invasion of personal space
   C   a tell-tale sign the person is lying

7. **If a person constantly interrupts you, it's ok to hold your hand up, and say with a smile, "Just a second, I'm not finished."**
   TRUE
   FALSE

8. It is no longer necessary or proper to recognize special positions, titles, or honorifics in professional engagements in the U.S. due to recent developments from equality, discrimination, social justice movements
   TRUE
   FALSE

9. The "traditional" time for afternoon tea is:
   A   2 o'clock
   B   3 o'clock
   C   4 o'clock

10. You can hand out a card or gift for Valentine's Day at the office
    TRUE
    FALSE

11. If you are being "toasted" at an occasion, you should acknowledge the honor and reciprocate by raising your glass with everyone
    TRUE
    FALSE

12. One must eat like an American in America, but use the Continental method when in Europe
    TRUE
    FALSE

13. In business, if you invite someone to lunch or dinner, you are expected to pay
    TRUE
    FALSE

14. A reasonable tip for a bellhop at a standard U.S. hotel is:
    A $2–$3 per bag
    B $5 per bag
    C   no longer customary or expected

15. John, a successful business professional, says he avoids approaching two people talking at a busy networking event, and looks for one person—or more than two; because:
    A   you get more business opportunities from 1 or 3+
    B   there's a chance you'd interrupt two people in a deep conversation
    C   the two people are likely to already know each other

16. During Louis XIV's reign, etiquets (signs) were displayed stating:
    A Keep Off The Grass
    B No Dueling In The Courtyard
    C Carriages Must Remain Mounted To Horses

17. What characteristic is NOT typical of most individuals from the "Millennial" generation?
    A prefer to own a business than be the top executive
    B gravitate toward businesses with a social mission
    C easily disconnect when not working

18. An RSVP with "regrets only" means:
    A you respond if you are unable to attend
    B you inform the host you received the invitation
    C you respond whether or not you are attending

19. When is it acceptable for you to move a place card set at a table?
    A never
    B when you need to sit with your child
    C when you have a disability that requires specific placement

20. It is unnecessary, and in fact—uncouth—to vocalize thanks to a service provider who is rendering an act he or she is paid to do
    TRUE
    FALSE

21. Wait staff should serve food:
    A with the left hand at the guest's left
    B with the right hand at the guest's right
    C with the right hand at the guest's left

22. A host may contact an invitee who has not responded to an RSVP
    TRUE
    FALSE

23. Plates, glassware, silverware should be removed from the right side of the guest
    TRUE
    FALSE

24. If your child is disruptive in a restaurant,
you should leave, even if your meal has been served
TRUE
FALSE

25. It is considered a breach or poor form to use your glass of water for a toast
TRUE
FALSE

26. Wait staff should serve beverages:
    A   with the left hand at the guest's left
    B   with the left hand at the guest's right
    C   with the right hand at the guest's right

27. You should never place a napkin on your chair
TRUE
FALSE

28. At a party, it's best to hold your drink in your left hand
TRUE
FALSE

29. It's tacky to ask for gifts, but a thoughtful gift registry is acceptable
TRUE
FALSE

30. Communication is improved when you directly address a care giver or
interpreter of individuals with physical challenges or disabilities
TRUE
FALSE

ANSWERS:

27. FALSE; 28. TRUE; 29. TRUE; 30. FALSE
22. TRUE; 23. TRUE; 24. TRUE; 25. FALSE; 26. C;
14. A; 15. B; 16. A; 17. C; 18. A; 19. A; 20. FALSE; 21. A;
8. FALSE; 9. C; 10. TRUE; 11. FALSE; 12. FALSE; 13. TRUE;
1. A; 2. TRUE; 3. TRUE; 4. FALSE; 5. C; 6. A; 7. TRUE;

Acknowledgments

While thinking about writing acknowledgments for this book, I realized just how many people have encouraged me and cheered me on during my etiquette career. I am enormously grateful to my teacher and mentor, Ms. Dorothea Johnson, founder of The Protocol School of Washington®. I will always be indebted to her for her unfailing support, encouragement, and guidance. I am also grateful to Ms. Pamela Eyring, President of the Protocol School of Washington, who continues Ms. Johnson's tradition of selfless assistance and advice to the graduates of PSOW®.

Many, many thanks to Dr. Giovanni Chimienti, Ms. Sandra Davis, Mr. Howard Feiertag, Dr. Murat Ferman, Mr. Michael Lannon, Dr. Joseph Meredith, and Dr. Raymond Smoot for believing in me and this project.

I am very grateful to Mr. James Harman, who designed the cover of the book. He is not only exceptionally creative, but remarkably patient!

Mr. Wesley Young, teacher; director; actor; playwright, and my co-author of the outdoor drama *Walk to Freedom: The Mary Draper Ingles Story*, kindly wrote the foreword to this book. Many thanks, dear Wesley, for your generosity of spirit, and your immense talent.

Also to my sons, Colonel Christian Harshberger, USMC, and Dr. Ted Harshberger who have encouraged me throughout this process, and who have always made their mother proud! And to my grandchildren, Brendan, Miriam, Avery and Cayden – this book is for you too.

Lots of dear friends and supporters have encouraged me in my writing and these include, but certainly are not limited to: Ms. Lois Timlin, whose discerning eye contributed so much to this project; my brother Dr. James Harvey, Ms. Nan Rogers, and Ms. Jennifer White. My grateful thanks to you all!

Finally, this book is a culmination of nearly nine years of writing a monthly column for The Valley Business FRONT. It would not have come to fruition without its editor and publisher, Mr. Tom Field. It is impossible to overstate my gratitude to him. The impact of his keen editorial eye; his consummate writing skills; his advice; his sense of humor, and his professionalism are incalculable. Thank you, Tom, for a wonderful journey!

Made in the USA
Columbia, SC
25 August 2019